The Mystery of Christ

A Scriptural Journey to Understanding the Anointing

Hugh Alexander Jackman

2012

The Mystery of Christ

A Scriptural Journey to Understanding the Anointing

Hugh Alexander Jackman

First Edition: June 2012

ISBN 978-1-9082931-6-9

© Hugh Alexander Jackman 2012

Hugh Alexander Jackman has asserted his rights under the Copyright, Designs and Patents act 1988 to be identified as the author of this work.

All rights reserved in all media. This book may not be copied, stored, transmitted or reproduced in any format or medium without specific prior permission from the authors or publisher.

Published by:
CGW Publishing
B 1502
PO Box 15113
Birmingham
B2 2NJ
United Kingdom
www.cgwpublishing.com

mail@cgwpublishing.com

Foreword

Get set for a spellbound adventure in a masterpiece of progressive revelation from the Bible. Hugh Jackman is a teacher's teacher, using his command of the English language and understanding of the scriptures to convey meanings that have been hidden in the word of God from many throughout the years.

If you wish to experience the profound in-depth simplicity of you as a believer and your relationship with Jesus, His anointing, and you as a son or daughter of the living God, follow the journey lined out in the chapters in The Mystery of Christ! You will find that each step of the journey, unto its final destination, will bring new light to heretofore unrecognized shades of darkness regarding you and your life in your Lord and Saviour, Jesus Christ.

The writings in this book are a must read for all serious Spirit-filled Christians in the world today. Block off some time, get a hot cup of coffee or tea, and settle in for the new empires of revelation waiting for you in The Mystery of Christ, a Scriptural Understanding of the Anointing. Well done, Pastor Jackman!

Benny Thomas

Best Selling Author and Teacher

Benny Thomas Ministries, U.S.A.

Preface

Every believer must have their own personal revelation of Christ! This book is dedicated to all who love the Lord with all of their hearts and seek to walk in the maximum of his presence even whilst here on the Earth.

Also to Seva, who has paid the price by ceaselessly releasing me to continue this work. It is dedicated to the enduring memory of those who have campaigned for the presence of God throughout the ages and serves only to continue their mandate of ministry in the Earth today.

Also to my parents, Maria, (and PG) Your guys are standing in God's perfect will with us. And of course, my Dad, Frank Irvine Jackman. A campaigner for right, a magistrate and a God fearing man, who encouraged me to think beyond the natural.

Contents

1. The Mystery of Christ 1
2. Revelation of Christ 9
3. The Glory of the Mystery 19
4. The Legal Chapter.....................................37
5. The Anti Anointing 55
6. Anointing in Us.......................................63
7. Burdens and Yokes 71
8. Defining the Anointing 81
9. The Healing Anointing.................................93
10. Living with the Anointing 107
11. The Presence of God.................................115
12. The Word of the Anointing...........................133
13. The Spirit of Adoption..............................157
14. The Power Chapter...................................177
15. Effects of the Anointing............................185
16. Enemies of the Anointing............................205
17. Proper Motivation...................................223
18. The Challenge 227
19. The Beautiful Spirit................................235
Thanks 239
Key Scriptures List....................................243
About the Author.......................................247

1. The Mystery of Christ

The Apostle Paul wrote in the 1ˢᵗ Chapter of Colossians:

23 if indeed you continue in the faith, grounded and steadfast, and are not moved away from the hope of the gospel which you heard, which was preached to every creature under heaven, of which I, Paul, became a minister.

24 I now rejoice in my sufferings for you, and fill up in my flesh what is lacking in the afflictions of Christ, for the sake of His body, which is the church,

25 of which I became a minister according to the stewardship from God which was given to me for you, to fulfil the word of God,

26 the mystery which has been hidden from ages and from generations, but now has been revealed to His saints.

27 To them God willed to make known what are the riches of the glory of this mystery among the Gentiles: which is Christ in you, the hope of glory.

28 Him we preach, warning every man and teaching every man in all wisdom, that we may present every man perfect in Christ Jesus.

A very great truth has become clear to me through the inspired writings of the Apostle Paul. I learned that whenever he, a man who received much revelation from God, used the word **"MYSTERY"**; he was speaking about something that had been divinely revealed to him by God. **(see, 2 Cor 12:2)**

Let's take a look at the divine order in which God has inspired Paul's writings. Notice: 1. The Riches, 2. Of the Glory 3. Of the Mystery. There are three distinct levels of revelation heading towards you right now Hallelujah!

Imagine a single corridor in front of you with only one door at the other end. You walk up to the door and notice that it is marked **"MYSTERY"**. You are intrigued, so you go through that door and immediately you come across another door, this one is marked **"GLORY OF THE MYSTERY"**. You go through that door and low and behold there is yet another door in front of you marked **"THE RICHES, OF THE GLORY, OF THE MYSTERY"**

Beloved friends, before we receive the "Riches" of the Glory of this Mystery", we must have our minds opened to see the "Glory of the Mystery", but before we can see that "Glory of the Mystery" we must understand the "Mystery". Hallelujah! Can you see it? The Mystery of Christ is revealed in layers, precept upon precept, line upon line! Now, your initial response may be to say that you fully understand this already and that Christ is no mystery to you at all. Whilst that may be true at present, the word mystery suggests that something deeper may be hidden or filed in secret, and that through your current attitude, you may be missing it, so think again!

A good word to anyone who thinks this way is: **Don't!** You can always learn something more with God! There is always something new that we can learn with Jesus Christ. In fact every time I think I have this revelation completely covered, the Holy Spirit drops another profound level in me that I hadn't considered before! There are deeper levels awaiting anyone with a teachable heart right now.

Christ in YOU

Before we talk about exactly what the word Christ is, let's firstly explore what it isn't. For simplicity sake therefore, the unravelling of the mystery of Christ begins with some simple "NOTS".

Christ is "NOT" the last name of Jesus! As simple as that may sound, you would be surprised at the number of people, even today, who have not considered the true meaning of the word Christ and, by its addition to the name Jesus, what it translates to us in both the Earth and Body of Christ today.

The second "not" is as follows:

Christ is "NOT" an English word! Yes, you can find it in the English language dictionary, however, it wasn't there originally.

Christ is a Greek word, translated from a Hebrew word, meaning to anoint or smear on. As Pastor of

House of Victory, I have found that many great truths are locked away from the body of Christ through poor or complete lack of translation. Our faith originated from Judaism, the faith of Israel, and as such, many of it's traditions and teachings are relevant yet sometimes unknown to us. This is especially true with the study of the Christ (the anointing). Translation is the key to understanding the great truth about Christ. We will greatly explore both those Greek and Hebrew terms later on, but for now let us settle on the statement "Christ simply means Anoint or Anointed", and the term "The Christ", means "The Anointed One". Now let's explore another relevant "NOT".

The Anointing is "NOT" chill bumps!

Or shivers, shouting, falling out or any other manifestation. This doesn't mean that these things are not associated with the anointing, in fact many times when the anointing is active, especially in church services, these manifestations are regular occurrences. However, they can all occur independently and without the true anointing being present. It is therefore, in my opinion, vital for the believer to know and understand what the anointing really is, learning where and how these manifestations fit in the picture.

As an illustration, I remember when my daughter Janah was a very small child. She was always asking questions about Jesus and God. One day I attempted to explain what the word Christ actually means and to my surprise, my four year old student summarised my teachings with childlike simplicity. She simply said "Jesus is smeared on me". Ignoring the fact that it came from four year old daughter, as you continue to read, you may find that this phrase will become clearer and even beneficial to you. It certainly was for me!

Now let us lay some vital background information on the subject. Courtesy of the Encyclopaedia Britannica we learn the following:

Many Eastern and Arabic religions believed that anointing carried a special mystical force or ability to transfer power, in fact Ancient Pharoah's had believed that the virtues of one killed could be transferred to survivors if the latter rubbed themselves with his caul-fat (the fat which surrounded his vital organs).

Also worth knowing is the practise of anointing a King or Queen for office. In fact at one time or another, most religions and faiths have used the process of anointing in ceremonial services.

Historical evidences may help us to understand the physical roots of anointing ceremonies, however, they will not help us to know the Spirit of God. Earlier I said that the prerequisite to understanding the mystery is to believe in Jesus Christ. May I ask you at this point. Do you believe? Have you ever invited him into your life to be your Lord and

Saviour? If you haven't, let me encourage you to do so now. You can pray any prayer from your heart, as long as you mean it sincerely, God will hear you, however the following words have brought many to a knowledge of Christ and salvation.

Prayer of Salvation

Dear Heavenly Father, I believe that you sent your son Jesus to die for my sins. That he died and rose again for my salvation, and that if I receive him in my heart I shall be saved. Therefore, according to your word, I confess my sins, renouncing the God of this world and receive Jesus now by faith. Thank you for saving me. Amen

Now as a believer in Jesus Christ you can ask the Lord to open your mind, removing any blindness so that the glorious light of the gospel of Jesus Christ should shine unto you.

2. Revelation of Christ

As I write these words, I am considering the years of study that the Lord has taken me through. How he initially revealed himself to me, and the subsequent teachings which brought the anointing to life in me. I have come to realise that the anointing is cumulative revelation building precept upon precept, line upon line. The revealing of Christ is, most certainly a divine process, taking us to a place of complete victory both in the Earth and in the life to come. In the sixteenth chapter of Matthew, a conversation is recorded between the Lord Jesus and his twelve Disciples in which we see Christ the mystery being revealed. It all began with Jesus asking the following question,

"Who do men say that I, the son of man, am?"

14 *So they said, Some say John the Baptist, some Elijah, and others Jeremiah or one of the prophets.*

15 *He said to them, But who do you say that I am?*

16 *Simon Peter answered and said, You are the Christ, the Son of the living God.*

17 *Jesus answered and said to him, Blessed are you, Simon Bar- Jonah, for flesh and blood has not revealed this to you, but My Father who is in heaven.*

18 *And I also say to you that you are Peter, and on this rock I will build My church, and the gates of Hades shall not prevail against it.*

19 *And I will give you the keys of the kingdom of heaven, and whatever you bind on earth will be bound in heaven, and whatever you loose on earth will be loosed in heaven.*

20 *Then He commanded His disciples that they should tell no one that He was Jesus the Christ.*

Simon sat quietly as the other disciples gave their answers to Jesus in verse 14. Simon (Peter) knew something, something no man had ever told him, he just knew it although it wasn't yet time for him to say what he knew.

Jesus gave absolutely no response when the disciples told him what the people were saying about him, however, he immediately wanted to know what those closest to him had to say in response to those incorrect statements. I believe Jesus could sense that Simon's silence wasn't brought about by ignorance or shyness, but by the awesome magnitude of the revelation that had been given to him directly from God.

Simon's answer was to produce a blessing unparalleled in the New Testament. It was to invoke a prophetic statement from our Lord Jesus that would echo throughout all time, serving as a mandate of power to every single member of the body of Christ.

Jesus spoke a blessing which, instantly released an incredible mantle of authority both on Simon

(Peter) and all of the generations, in time to come, to whom this word would be revealed and that includes both you and I today!

The Lord Jesus instantly declared a timeless prophetic word not only to Simon Peter but to the entire Church to come, HALLELUJAH!.

He said in no uncertain terms, that it is upon this revelation, or the revealing of himself in this manner, that he will build his Church. God the Father revealing the son of God in the hearts of each and every believer would produce unparalleled growth of the Kingdom of God in the Earth. Notice also: He called it **HIS CHURCH**. And he said that **HIS CHURCH**, *armed* with this rock solid revelation, would stand up against the very gates of hell.

Through this scripture we know for certain exactly what the Church of Jesus Christ is supposed to be comprised of today. It is to be the Church born of revelation truth from the Father God. Walking in the absolute authority of God, having the keys, *(or authority)* to access the things of the Kingdom of Heaven. It is a church that is able to declare matters of this world both lawful and unlawful (Binding and Loosing with the authority of God) here in the Earth, with the gates of Hell not being able to prevail in any form against it.

The Word has been spoken and cannot be reversed, therefore we, as the church, must by revelation, appropriate and receive it by faith. It is the Lord's will for us to walk in the Victory which he promised through this Word.

Now, If you are in agreement with what you have just read, it is imperative that we now consider most carefully, the following question:

What exactly did Simon (Peter) say?

Lets examine his words carefully. Simon said **"You are the CHRIST, the son of the Living God"**. Or did he?

Looking carefully again, we notice, that Simon (Peter) was a Jew and as such, he didn't speak Greek. By default, we must assume that he spoke Hebrew.

Now CHRIST is a Greek word, so although the text was translated this way, Simon didn't actually say you are the "CHRIST". Simon used the original Hebrew word for Christ, which is, "Messiah", this was later translated into the word **CHRIST** by Greeks who interpreted the account into their own language (See ACTS 11:26). Translation is key when it comes to understanding the mystery of Christ.

Imagine this thought. If we can determine exactly what Simon actually said, and if we can say it with the same conviction and belief that he did, it follows that we should receive the same resultant blessing from Jesus that Simon received!

The presence of God on Simon (who became Peter) was so mighty at times the bible records that his very shadow healed sick people that he passed on the roadside. Likewise, I believe that the anointing on our lives can be just as powerful as Peter's! Perhaps with even greater results...

ACTS 5:14 *And believers were increasingly added to the Lord, multitudes of both men and women, 15 so that they brought the sick out into the streets and laid them on beds and couches, that at least the shadow of Peter passing by might fall on some of them. 16 Also a multitude gathered from the surrounding cities to Jerusalem, bringing sick people and those who were tormented by unclean spirits, and they were all healed.*

So what did Simon actually say? Simon said, **YOU ARE THE MESSIAH**, the **Son of the living God**. Notice, he didn't say, I think you are. He said YOU ARE. Simon was fully convinced and persuaded that what he was saying was fact, and no opinion of man was ever going to change that. This attitude connected with Jesus in such a way, that he instantly, perceiving Simon differently, changed his name from Simon (meaning sand), to Peter, meaning fragment of a huge rock.

Through this prophetic act, I believe Jesus was saying that this revelation is rock-like, it's as solid as a rock. Since you are the one who said it, your character has changed from sand to being a rocky (Rock Solid) type of believer.

From now on, we will refer to Simon the same way Jesus did. We can now call him Peter because we know why Jesus called him Peter:

Why was it, that although there were at least twelve men in that room, only Peter got what I call the "rocky" revelation? There must have been something about Peter's character, which gave way to the unveiling of his mind. Christ was, to everybody else in that room, a mystery.

I was born again, for at least a year before I began to receive the revelation of Christ. I will never forget the way it happened. I was already a Christian attending church, reading my bible etc. but I had not yet found the true purpose for my life. I was enjoying my faith but for myself and nobody else.

I believe there are many Christians today who are just like I was then, basically self centred. The revelation of Christ is as much a mystery to them as it was to the other eleven Disciples in Peter's day. The revealing of Christ did for me, exactly what it did for Peter. It changed my identity and gave me a new purpose for living.

I began to understand that being born again was more than just falling out, having wonderful visions and speaking in tongues. Although I did plenty of all three in my first year of being saved! I began to realise that God has a purpose for every Christian to be become the "rocky" foundation stones upon which Jesus can build His Church.

UNDERSTANDING THE MYSTERY

Saint Peter said you are the "Messiah", the son of the living God. Let's take this one bite at a time. Who was this Messiah and what does this word really mean? Most of us think that the translation for Messiah or Christ, is simply, the son of the living God because Peter followed the title with those words. We tend to read it like this: "You are the Christ *meaning* the son of the living God". If we are to find out what Peter really said, we must do an in depth study of the word Messiah. We can then fully understand exactly what the words meant to Peter when he said them.

As I mentioned earlier, the early translations of the Hebrew Torah, the old testament, were translated into Greek and from there, into English. So for the scholars among us, here are the literal translations.

HEBREW: *mashiyach*[4899], *maw-shee'-akh; meaning: anointed; usually a consecrated person (as a king, priest, or saint); spec. the Messiah:--anointed, Messiah.*

GREEK: CHRISTOS, *the idea of contact; to smear or rub with oil, i.e. to consecrate to an office or religious service: -- anoint.*

ENGLISH: ANOINTED *Middle English via Anglo-French anoint (adj.) from Old French enoint, past part. of enoindre, from Latin inungere (as in-2, ungere unct- 'smear with oil')*

You are the Messiah!

Peter said you are the Messiah meaning you are the Anointed One. He is saying there is something on you, and it's not of this world but I can see it, it has been revealed to me!

Now, the Mystery is over for Peter but likewise its over for us. We can go ahead and start translating the word CHRIST every time we see it. We can translate the words Jesus Christ to now read either Jesus the Anointed or Jesus the Anointed one.

Stop right now and consider these words very carefully, the proper definition of CHRIST is to rub on, or smear on. You may say that doesn't sound very amazing, or even very religious! But remember, the Mystery comes first then the glory then THE RICHES - Read on.

3. The Glory of the Mystery

The word glory used here means to honour! So let us now give honour to the mystery by taking a deeper step into it. You see, many times we fail to honour the mystery of Christ, even when we understand what it means! We need to dig deeper, prayerfully in order to receive the blessing contained therein. Glory to God in the Highest! By now, you know, Christ means to smear or rub on. Now that we understand the word Christ, we can proceed to those deeper depths and higher heights. If you will, for a moment, try to think of the word Christ as a concept and not a name. The concept being: "ANOINTING". This concept can be compared to the words, "painting or smearing".

At this point I wish to introduce the concept of the Trinity, not because I wish to create division within the Church but because without this concept, we cannot fully grasp the meaning of Christ. When I became a Christian, another truth I became aware of is that sometimes the body of Christ can be divided over apparently central doctrinal issues. One of the primary issues being The Trinity. Some believe in its existence whilst others do not. Prominent Ministers take either one side or another, denouncing the other person's position as erroneous. As the writer of this book, I can actually identify with both arguments, let me explain why. As a Prophet I can identify with the non Trinitarian position because prophetically speaking, Jesus said

"If you have seen me, you have also seen the Father" (John 14:7)

However, speaking as a Bible student and teacher on the subject of the anointing, you would have to ignore three quarters of the New Testament and large parts of the Old Testament in order to embrace the theological argument against the Trinity.

As an illustration, imagine if you will, a beach ball the size of a football pitch with four distinctive colours, red, white, blue and green. It is in the middle of a football pitch where the supporters of each colour can only see their respective colour. Red can only see red, white can only see white, blue can only see blue and green can only see green. Each can only see from their own perspective but not from his neighbours. Beach ball truth is only perceived when the ball is raised above the stadium, then, all of the supporters can see all four colours at the same time. Likewise it is not until we see the Gospel from a Heavenly prospective that we can enjoy the fullness of what it has to offer us. I pray that whatever your doctrinal position is, that you may continue this book to its conclusion as it is based only on the word of God which after all is the final authority in all of our lives.

Understanding the Trinity, The Father, The Son and The Holy Spirit is an essential element in grasping the mystery of Christ. We were made in the image of God. Father, Son & Holy Spirit, see Genesis Chapter

1:26. God said, let us make man, in our own image. God speaks about himself in the plural not in the singular! God was not talking to some other Gods. He was speaking and referring to his own triune nature. Because we were created in the image of God, it makes sense that we must also have been created as triune beings. There are several scriptures which bear witness to this fact. Look at the following scripture carefully:

I Cor 6:20 *For you were bought at a price; therefore glorify God in your body and in your spirit, which are God's.*

According to this scripture, we have both body and spirit. Since we know we have a mind, we can conclude that all three are present in our triune nature. Think about it like this. If you are born again, you are a spirit being with a mind, living in a body.

The key thing to remember here is that the Word of God, (The message of the anointing) brings the believer to the point of being able to identify their triune nature more perfectly, without the word of God we will be completely unable to see it. Hebrews 4:12, illustrates this perfectly.

Here you can see the three elements of man divided by the word. Firstly: the Spiritual "Soul and Spirit", then the Physical "Joints and Marrow", and finally, the intellectual "thoughts and intents of the heart". The Word of God which you are reading right now is revealing to you your true nature. If you are open to receive it, you may also become aware of your triune nature. Without this revelation, it will be difficult to comprehend the way in which the anointing operates. The anointing has different effects on our mind, spirit and soul. This is the reason why many are confused about the anointing and its power in our lives today. The Apostle Paul understood this revelation and taught us about it in the book of Romans Chapter seven. In dealing with the subject of sin, he was able to say, it is not I that commits it but sin that dwells in me. He also speaks of a war in his members.

(22) For I delight in the law of God according to the inward man. (23) But I see another law in my members, warring against the law of my mind, and bringing me into captivity to the law of sin which is in my members. (24) O wretched man that I am! Who will deliver me from this body of death? (25) I thank God-through Jesus Christ our Lord!

So then, with the mind I myself serve the law of God, but with the flesh the law of sin.

You can see clearly here the writer makes mention of his own triune nature, the Mind, the Body or flesh and the inward man, all within one sentence!

In the early days of our ministry, I decided to turn our spare bedroom into a TV studio. In order to do this, I had to purchase some special blue paint. I began painting the room at the top of one wall, I reached half way down the wall and then decided that since the lower area would be covered by set I wouldn't bother to waste the paint. In the short term the set served its purpose, but later on we needed a spare bedroom again. In spite of my wife's repeated requests to make the wall one colour or another I never did get around to finishing that wall. After that time, quite naturally, I gained the reputation of being a poor painter. I promised that I would do the job but simply failed to get the job done. What I should have done, is gone down to the paint store, bought a tin of magnolia and a brush applied it to the wall in perfect thin layers repeatedly until my previously botched job had been hidden, but I didn't. Likewise, if you think of your previous understanding of the word "Christ", as my half completed wall and this new revelation that you are reading about as a fresh coat of magnolia. You will then need to continually apply a fresh coat over the previous layer until all you can see is a perfect coating of truth.

My painting illustration is an apt one because the word paint allows us to see the Anointing with fresh eyes. Picture me, if you will, wearing my overall, and a paint brush in my hand. I am ready to paint or anoint the wall. I am therefore the painter of the Anointer. Now picture the tin of Magnolia on the floor in front of me with a perfect bristled paint brush balanced on the lid. This is my new wall colour or the Anointing. Now picture my untidily previously painted bedroom wall, blue at the top, white at the bottom. It is about to become Anointed!

Understanding the concept of Christ, like my former spare bedroom, requires the visualisation of three distinct entities. Since Christ means to Anoint, like Paint, we must break the word down to its three principle characteristics which are:

1. The Anointer (someone must be doing the anointing)
2. The Anointed (someone must be receiving anointing)
3. The Anointing (Anointing must have, or be, substance)

The Anointer, Anointed and his Anointing

These three are all clearly represented in the book of Acts Chapter 10:34 where Peter, years after receiving the revelation of Christ, is now armed with his prophetic word, and is preaching the message of Jesus the Anointed with power. He proclaimed that God anointed Jesus of Nazareth with the Holy Ghost and with power.

Acts 10:34 *Then Peter opened his mouth and said: In truth I perceive that God shows no partiality. (35) But in every nation whoever fears Him and works righteousness is accepted by Him. (36) The word which God sent to the children of Israel, preaching peace through Jesus Christ - He is Lord of all - (37) that word you know, which was proclaimed throughout all Judea, and began from Galilee after the baptism which John preached: (38) how God anointed Jesus of Nazareth with the Holy Spirit and with power, who went about doing good and healing all who were oppressed by the devil, for God was with Him.*

Are you able to see the how the Holy Trinity are all embodied in the concept of Anointing. The Word of God (The Holy Bible) here beginning in verse 38, clearly depicts God, the Father of our Lord Jesus, as the <u>Anointer</u>. Now we know that Christ means Anointed, therefore Jesus <u>Christ</u>, is the <u>Anointed</u>.

Notice, the Anointing is not a thing like my paint. He is the third person of the trinity, none other than the Holy Spirit. The power mentioned here is associated with the Holy Spirit because the Holy Spirit brings the power of God into our lives. We will talk more about that later.

Now we can see that the word CHRIST isn't just a name but it is in fact, an incredible God designed concept incorporating the presence of all three members of the God head dwelling in a human being. The anointer is anointing his anointed.

If we read on in the book of Acts, we can see the fulfilment of the prophecy, which Jesus spoke over Peter's rocky revelation back in Matthew 16.

44 *While Peter yet spoke these words, the Holy Ghost fell on all who heard it..*

The Lord Jesus said, upon this word of the anointing, he will build his church. Here we can clearly see, the anointing (The Holy Spirit and Power) is falling upon everyone who heard this word. Notice Peter has not changed his confession from Matthew chapter 16, which we read earlier, in fact it is fair to say that he has based his entire ministry on what Jesus told him! Remember, he said you are the rock and upon this rock I will build my church transliterated as "On this revelation, I will build my church". Everywhere Peter went, he preached exactly the same message. God, the anointer, anointing his anointed, Jesus Christ. Remember that this is exactly what Peter said in answer to the question, which Jesus asked of the Disciples. Who do men say that I the son of man am? Then Peter answered, "You are the Christ, the son of the living God". Stop and think about that for a moment, because through this amazing chapter of the book of Acts, we have found three great truths. Firstly this was Peter's message. Secondly, this was the Gospel message. And thirdly this should be our message in the Church of Jesus Christ today. That is the glory of the mystery.

What message did Jesus Christ preach?

Did you know that when Jesus walked the Earth as a man, he preached this exact same message? He not only taught it, he demonstrated it everywhere he went.

In the book of Isaiah chapter 61, there was a prophecy given. It was a fearsome prophecy. It was an amazing prophecy. It was a Messiah defining prophecy.

The Jewish people knew that when the messiah would come - he would not only speak these words with authority, but he would live the prophecy, demonstrating the power of God for all to see.

The Lord Jesus didn't disappoint in this regard, for we see him acting out the words of Isaiah's prophecy in the Earth perfectly throughout his ministry.

I want to draw our attention to a specific moment in His ministry where we see a man who was born blind receive his sight. We are going to break this miracle down line by line because as we unpack the hidden meanings stored within these verses, we will receive a greater understanding of the anointing power on our own lives! Let's turn to the book of John chapter 9 vs. 1 and begin there.

We see the Lord Jesus passing by a man who was blind from birth. At this point, His disciples ask Him a question. "Rabbi, who sinned, this man or his parents, that he was born blind"?

Now, if you analyse this carefully you will find that this was a loaded question. How could the man have sinned before he was born?

Meditate on that for a moment before you move on to the next verse. Ready to move on? OK, let's continue. Indeed, That was an amazing question but even more fascinating was the answer that Lord Jesus gave to it. "Neither this man nor his parents sinned but that the works of God be made manifest in him". I failed to understand this scripture for years until I began to look at it from the standpoint of the anointing. What did Jesus mean by the words "the works of God"?

I believe he was referring to the anointing. I believe he was talking about the God's perfect plan of salvation for mankind which He was about to demonstrate through the healing of this blind man.

Understanding the trinity, the word has been spoken.

When I travel to the USA, I sometimes like to visit a burger bar or two, generally, if you are looking for a burger with everything on it you would order the works! Interestingly, this is exactly what we are about to see in this miracle! It has got everything in it!

Now, first of all we must understand that this man represents all of mankind. The condition of blindness represents the sin condition which we are all born into.

Now notice verse six.

When He said these things He spat on the ground and made clay with the saliva, then he anointed the eyes of the blind man with the clay.

What was the Lord doing? He spits on the ground and now I picture him making putty in his hands by stirring the spittle and the dust together. Just try to picture it now. Stir your finger around the palm of your other hand, until you picture Jesus doing the same. It will help you to receive the full picture here.

Now, let me ask you this question. Have you ever heard of DNA?

Check out this definition: It is defined as a nucleic acid that carries the genetic information in the cell and is capable of self-replication and synthesis of RNA. DNA consists of two long chains of nucleotides twisted into a double helix and joined by hydrogen bonds between the complementary bases adenine and thymine or cytosine and guanine. The sequence of nucleotides determines individual hereditary characteristics. In simple terms, DNA carries the entire physical formula for the creature from which it came.

Forensic science today needs only a small sample of a persons saliva to determine the DNA characteristics of the human being from which the sample came. In other words, the complete molecular pattern of the entire man is contained in his saliva. People today are convicted and sent to prison based on DNA evidence alone.

According to the book of Genesis, God made man from the dust of the ground. So what do we have thus far? The DNA of the sinless man being mixed with the dust from which God created Adamic man. Hmm, We will discuss this further in the next chapter.

This, my dear friends, is the ultimate picture of the anointing. I hope you can see it, the DNA of God combined with the flesh of man. As Jesus anoints the eyes of the blind man, a credible miracle takes place. Likewise when God's anointing comes upon our lives, amazing things begin to happen to us also.

Now as I said earlier, the blindness represents sin. When Jesus anointed him, the blindness disappeared. He was no longer the blind man. He was now a new creature in Christ! People who had watched him beg daily for years simply couldn't recognise him any more. Likewise, when Jesus anointed you and I, the sin condition disappeared! You became a new creature, with a new DNA. Imperfect man overlaid with perfection. This, therefore is a picture of the blood of Jesus working powerfully against the sin condition in our lives.

Let's see what happened after this point.

As long as I am in the world, I am the light of the world. (6) When he had thus spoken, he spat on the ground, and made clay of the spittle, and he anointed the eyes of the blind man with the clay, (7) And said unto him, Go, wash in the pool of Siloam, (which is by interpretation, Sent.) He went his way therefore, and washed, and came seeing

Let's unpack some more meanings here.

The washing represents both the Word of God and baptism. both of which are necessary for anointing to take place.

"Siloam" means "sent". This is a picture of the apostolic aspect of the anointing. You are not anointed for yourself only, but that you would bring the good news of Christ to those who are bereft. As the account continues we see the man who was blind being questioned by the authorities of the day. He answered them with great wisdom. This is a picture of the mind of Christ which we receive when we receive him through the anointing.

The Pharisees failed miserably trying to catch the man out with their clever questions. For me, the once useless blind man now becomes a biblical hero, displaying boldness, intelligence and even a bit of humour. He becomes a preacher and his words prick the hearts of the leaders who heard him. So much so that eventually, completely frustrated, they put him out of the synagogue where the Lord Jesus finds him.

What follows is the most significant element of this entire passage. For the first time recorded anywhere in Scripture, the Lord Jesus Christ reveals himself to the blind man as the Son of God. This must be significant to us for this is something that our Lord Jesus never did ordinarily. For legal reasons, He was most careful never to reveal his identity as the son of God. Here, however he reveals all.

This is a picture of what happens to us after the anointing has come upon our lives. Through the Holy Spirit, we not only have wisdom, but we inherit a greater knowledge of both the Son of God and the fact that we are also His sons.

Beloved friend, although you and I were born with Adamic flesh. We have also being reborn by and through the Spirit of God.

His DNA is now smeared on our natural bodies. His supernatural anointing is on our natural flesh. This is why we struggle in the flesh periodically. Combining the flesh of man with the DNA of God is a humongous task only achievable through the anointing.

I pray that your knowledge of Christ, the anointing, will increase with every chapter of this book. I pray that the eyes of your understanding will be opened. That wisdom and knowledge of your sonship shall become clearer and clearer to you. That the wisdom of the highest order will come and dwell in your heart by and through the anointing.

The story of the Messiah is a continuing one. Beginning with the Lord Jesus, this is a never ending series of accounts which you and I as the body of God's anointed are now writing in the Earth.

Let's delve deeper still... Going back to the book of Acts, we find the following words:

Acts 10:37 *says That word, I say, ye know, which was published throughout all Judaea, and began from Galilee, after the baptism which John preached; 38 How <u>God</u> anointed <u>Jesus of Nazareth</u> with the <u>Holy Ghost</u> and with power: who went about doing good, and healing all that were oppressed of the devil; for God was with him.*

As you can see, the prophecy in Isaiah 61 echoes marvellously here in the book of Acts.

Let's examine our passage very carefully. Notice in verse 37 we are told that "the Word" was first preached in Galilee after the baptism of John.

Wouldn't it be great if we could just open our Bibles right now and see exactly the same message recorded in perfect clarity, after John preached, in Galilee? Interestingly, we can! Just turn your attention to the book of Luke Chapters 3 and 4 and the entire account is faithfully recorded. The beginning of Luke 3 records the account of John the Baptist and his baptism of repentance. In verse 21, we see the Lord Jesus being baptised. In the beginning of chapter 4 we see Jesus turning up at

Galilee, (after the baptism of John), he goes into the synagogue there, opens the scroll and finds the place where it is written.

Luke 4:18 *The Spirit of the Lord is upon me, because he hath anointed me to preach the gospel to the poor; he hath sent me to heal the broken-hearted, to preach deliverance to the captives, and recovering of sight to the blind, to set at liberty them that are bruised,*

19 *To preach the acceptable year of the Lord.*

20 *And he closed the book, and he gave it again to the minister, and sat down. And the eyes of all them that were in the synagogue were fastened on him.*

21 *And he began to say unto them, This day is this scripture fulfilled in your ears.*

Can you see it? The Spirit of the Lord is upon me because he has anointed me... The Bible clearly shows us the three elements involved in the process of anointing in this passage. Let me outline them again. The Spirit of the Lord is the Anointing. The Lord God is the Anointer. Jesus is the Anointed one.

Today, if you are born again. You and I are the body of Christ. We are anointed with the Holy Spirit, by God who is the anointer who makes this all possible.

By faith, you are the genuine article! Anointed, legally adopted into the family of Messiah in the Earth. Hallelujah!

4. The Legal Chapter

The Case of the Devil Versus The Lord

The more I examine the Scriptures on this subject, the more I have become convinced that the anointing is not just a matter of religious practises but in fact it is a matter of legality. Yes, it does speak of power and deliverance but this is the result of the anointing not the anointing itself. The Anointing is the Holy Spirit but his presence in the Earth can be viewed from a legal perspective with great revelatory benefits.

Yes friend the anointing is a legal issue, it was necessary because God is absolutely righteous and must always operate within his own predefined rules of holiness and uprightness. Before you make any conclusions, please allow me to present the entire case to you.

I would suggest that you take each thought separately and examine them carefully with the aid of the Holy Spirit. Scrutinise the Scriptures until you are completely satisfied that my conclusions are in fact, God breathed. This will really help you to receive from the rest of this book.

So, firstly let us break down the legal issue.

The Legal Background

God our Father is the Holy God. He is Holy and righteous. His nature is blameless, morally sound and perfectly upright because He is the first cause of law and everything that is righteous in the world. After God the Father made the Earth in the first chapter of Genesis, He put the man in it and gave him total and complete authority over it.

This first man's name was Adam. From the rib of the man, he produced a woman to be his wife. Adam named her Eve. This first couple had complete and total supremacy over the Earth. In fact, to put it simply they were like Gods in the Earth. Now when the Serpent saw the power, the authority and the favour that these Earth Gods Adam and Eve had, he sought to relieve them of it. The method which he employed was a subtle one. We have come to know this today as temptation. In Adam and Eve's case the temptation was shrouded in deceit.

This is because satanic temptation is never as simple as it appears to be. The enemy very often tricks us by presenting a temptation to us without declaring the hidden consequences of succumbing to it. This was the case with the first couple who inadvertently brought not only a curse on themselves but on every generation after them.

The entire family of mankind will, after this point be brought under the curse of original sin.

The obvious question at this point is, Why didn't God just kill Adam, Eve and the serpent and start over again? Good question! I believe the answer can be found in exercising an in-depth study of God's righteousness. Let us unpack this thought together right now.

As I have already stated, God is the first cause of all righteousness and that he operates within his own predefined rules of uprightness. Since He had given the Earth's supremacy to Adam and Eve it would have been unrighteous by his own standard of righteousness to attempt to take it back.

We see this fact illustrated in the biblical account of Jacob and Esau. Consider Jacob, who became the father of the twelve tribes of Israel. He gained the blessing from his father by deceitful methods. Later, when he wrestled with God he received the blessing from the Lord also! Once the blessing was given by his father Isaac, it could not be retracted, neither by man or by God. (Genesis 27)

To illustrate this point a little bit further let me use the example of a birthday gift. Let us imagine that you wanted to give a gift to your best friend but you did not know exactly what to buy them. You might choose to give them a monetary gift specifying that they should use it to buy themselves a lovely present. Let us imagine further that upon receiving the cash gift your best friend decided, instead of purchasing a nice gift, to pay a very important bill. Since this was considered to be more of a priority.

Upon hearing this you may think you have reason to be quite upset. However in God's eyes it would be unrighteous for you to do so. The reason being is that when you hand a gift over to someone else, you no longer have the right to dictate what they are to do with it. If I were to give you a gift and you were to give it away to someone else, you would be perfectly within your right to do so. I may not be happy about it but I must accept it because I gave it to you unconditionally. You see that is the nature of true giving, it is completely unconditional.

When God gave the supremacy of the Earth to Adam and Eve he commanded them to have dominion over it and to subdue it, along with every living creature within it. The serpent knew that if it could get them by and through sin, to fail in this commandment that they (that is Adam and Eve) would lose their right to rule.

The serpent's dastardly plan succeeded and they were reduced in rank from Earthly Gods to mere living beings. (1Cor 15:45) The Serpent, by default or by a legal loophole gained Earth supremacy from them. They inadvertently handed over their Earthly authority to satan.

There was however another consequence to this entire scenario.

God's word

In the book of Genesis chapter 3 verse 14 God pronounces his sentence upon the Serpent.

14 *So the Lord God said to the serpent:*

Because you have done this, You are cursed more than all cattle, And more than every beast of the field; On your belly you shall go, And you shall eat dust All the days of your life.15 And I will put enmity Between you and the woman, And between your seed and her Seed; He shall bruise your head, And you shall bruise His heel.

Notice *her Seed*. It is this sentence that lays the legal foundation for our understanding of the anointing that was to come. Although it was upon the man that authority was originally placed, it would be the Seed of the Woman that would ultimately bring about the destruction of satan's authority.

Paul wrote in the Book of Romans that it was through one man that sin entered the race of mankind. (Romans 5:12) Again, there was no mention about the woman, only the man. It is possible to deduce therefore, that sin has been passed through the ages from one man to the next, from generation to generation. But notice, by God's specific wording of the curse, it doesn't apply to woman kind in simple terms this means that although she is under it, because of her husband, she doesn't posses the ability to reproduce it!

The Biblical rule of Seeds is that they will always reproduce after their own kind. Since the Woman has no seed she is unable to reproduce the sin condition. She can only pass it on.

One reason for this is found in the book of Leviticus chapter 17, which teaches us that the life is in the blood. Let me illustrate this with another analogy. When a plane crashes, the search begins for the indestructible black box. This very tough box records every relevant and significant function of the plane and of its operators throughout a flight therefore it will hold vital information about what happened before the crash. Every Earth creature's blood does exactly the same. Through a unique system of chemical nucleotides and DNA, every significant factor about the species is recorded!

Now, that being the case, we may also assume that lack of life or even a curse may also be recorded in the blood. In fact, many hereditary diseases are diagnosed by a study of a person's blood and family history. In fact, medical science upholds the theory that every human child inherits the blood characteristics of his or her father, not the mother. Women may pass on looks, hair colour and a few habits but that's about it!

Adams bloodline had been contaminated by sin and therefore it follows that every generation after him also had contaminated blood flowing through its veins. This also included righteous Israel.

Generations after God pronounced the Curse, according to the Bible genealogies recorded in both Matthew and Luke, a son of Israel was born. He was a righteous man named Joseph. He was to be betrothed to a virgin girl whose name was Mary. Mary was no ordinary girl. She was literally the Word of prophecy from the Garden coming to pass in the Earth! She was the Woman from whom a seed would be born that would crush the head of the Serpent.

Although Joseph was to marry her, his seed was not to touch her as yet, for the Holy thing that was to be born of her was to walk as a man in the Earth whilst yet being the Son of God. In order to do that there must be no trace of Adamic blood in his veins. Joseph watched his wife conceive a child without having touched her physically. That alone is a subject for much further discussion but we will not attempt to do so now. Suffice to say that God sent an Angel to assure him of the validity of Mary's virginity.

So why is this a Legal Issue?

This was a legal issue firstly because the descendants of the entire Adamic bloodline are held under the authority of the God of this World. It follows then, that the Messiah, since he was born for the purpose of dethroning him, absolutely cannot be born under this authority.

The second reason is simply that if God had sent man's saviour in the form of another Earthly God, he would have given the God of this World reason to accuse him of unrighteousness. Now some of you may feel that I am pushing it by suggesting that satan brings accusations against our God so let us turn to scripture to investigate the validity of this argument also.

The Plaintiff's case

The book of Job records two occasions when the Sons of God came before their Heavenly Father and it is recorded that satan came along with them. He comes not as a worshipper but as a spy and an accuser. God allows him to come and make representation before him. He even invites him to speak on the subject of his servant Job. God is fully aware that satan watches the activity of the blessed ones in the Earth. Believer that includes you and I! Notice however, satan doesn't even attempt to discuss the validity of Jobs righteousness but instead he hurls railing accusations at God himself. You have blessed him, you have protected him. You have put a hedge around him! Amazingly, as a result of these accusations, he is permitted to exercise tests against Job to prove that it was in fact Job's own righteousness that brought the reward of God's favour and protection. This scripture alone, clearly portrays the enemy's accusatory nature along with his blatant disregard for the righteousness of God.

From the moment that the Serpent heard God's pronouncement upon him, he began to search the Earth for that one who would be born of the Woman. He knew that he would be human but that he would have to have Godly characteristics. What really concerned him was that he would be armed with the ability to crush his head of authority. Over the centuries, he used many unGodly men to annihilate every possible qualifier. He obliterated entire generations in Moses day, again in Christ's day and some may even say also in Hitler's day. He is looking for one who is to be born in the World with the ability to destroy his power on Earth.

According to the Word of God, the Lord Jesus was born of the virgin Mary. He was to walk in the Earth as a natural man so that his legal status could not be challenged by the Devil and his minions.

But how was a mere man to bring about the destruction of the kingdom of darkness on the Earth? Since he was flesh and blood and could not walk in his Godly powers. How was he to achieve this insurmountable task?

In truly theatrical terms I present to you God's prophetic solution to this legal quandary, the answer my friend lies not blowing in the wind but in the ruach outpouring of the Anointing of the Holy Spirit.

The Judge's Verdict

satan's dominion is limited to the realms of the flesh therefore he has absolutely no authority over the spirit. By God's wisdom, therefore it is in the realm of the spirit of man that God has chosen for the anointing of the Holy Spirit to dwell. Jesus told us not to heap treasure where the moth can eat it, but heap up your treasures in the realm of the spirit! (Matthew 6:19)

Whilst it certainly would have been illegal for God to send another physical God to dethrone satan, the Holy Spirit has always been present in the Earth. So there was no need to send him. He was here in the Earth, way before the Devil witnessing his every move. In fact, from the very beginning, the Spirit of God moved on the face of the waters. Throughout biblical history the Holy Spirit came on men to give them victory over their enemies. Likewise it is the Holy Spirit that will descend upon Jesus the man after the baptism of John and give him total power and authority in Earth. It is the very same Holy Spirit that the Lord promises to send back for every believer in the book of John described in Greek as Allos Parakletos or Another Comforter (John 14:16).

The Bible tells us that God was in Christ reconciling the world unto himself.

(2 Corinthians 5:19) God was literally in the Anointing (We must always translate the word Christ into the original language and meaning: Messiah, meaning to smear upon, we will discuss more about this later. God was literally in the anointing of the Holy Spirit) so although we see Jesus walking in the Earth as a man, he literally walked with God.

Final Arguments

Since this is a legal issue, we should make our closing arguments perfectly clear. Firstly:

Has either Jesus or God the Father broken any Heavenly laws? No, in fact our Lord Jesus acknowledged the fact that satan had supremacy in the Earth, right up until the point that he went to the cross. After the cross, he stated that all authority had been given unto him. During his time of ministry, He said that the God of this World had blinded the minds of those who do not believe. This was a total acknowledgement of the enemy's Earth status.

Jesus said in the book of John Chapter 14 verse 30, that the prince of this world is coming but he has nothing in me. I believe that he was referring to the absence of the sinful blood of Adam, meaning that satan was unable to exercise any authority over the Lord. Since he was a man, it was therefore legal for him to take the place of our saviour in the Earth.

Did Jesus come to the Earth as God? No! If you carefully analyse his speech, Jesus only referred to his own deity in the third person! In other words, he would only quote someone else's reference to the fact. The term "son of Man" on the other hand, is used almost exclusively by Christ, occurring some 87 times in the New Testament. The term Son of God conversely occurs some 19 times, mostly used by the accuser but never by Christ himself in the first person. Isn't this interesting? According to what is recorded in Scripture, Christ rarely used the term. He was careful to use legally correct speech at all times. So didn't Christ know that he was the Son of God? Don't be silly! Of course he did! He just didn't say it because it was a legal issue. There were minions listening and hanging onto every word that escaped his mouth.

Did you further know that Miranda, the legal terms which must be used when one is arrested by the police or authorities, was first uttered by Christ? Miranda states:

"Anything that you say maybe taken down and used in evidence against you".

Jesus Christ in the book of Matthew 12:37 said, *by your words you shall be justified and by your words, condemned!*

Although many scripture identify him as the Son of God, he rarely actually came out and said it himself. I believe this was because Jesus was acutely aware of the laws of God, he was careful not to break them. Hallelujah!

Conversely, as I have shown, the Lord called himself Son of man many more times in scripture. He was stating his case clearly and abundantly. He is legally here and there is nothing whatsoever, that the devil can do about it.

Did Jesus exercise Godly powers on Earth illegally? No, in fact according to the Bible, which is the only source of reliable data on the subject, he didn't exercise any earthly power or authority until he had been endowed with the Holy Spirit. Furthermore, he told his disciples to wait in Jerusalem until they also had been endued with power from the most high before beginning their ministries! Why? Because the authority of God is in the anointing of the Holy Spirit. His disciples were not acting in their own name but in the name and the authority of Jesus.

Is it legal for believers to walk in the authority of the anointing? Yes! Absolutely yes! This is the most exciting news for us because through the Anointing, the Lord sets a new precedent in the Earth. In fact, all those who have received Jesus are born of his Spirit having become Sons of God. (John 1:11) They, by the investment of the Holy Spirit, have come out from under the authority system of this world. Through the anointing, they have come under the governance of the Kingdom of God. Hallelujah!

The Anointing, (The presence of God in man through the Holy Spirit) gave Christ total authority in the Earth. Christ walked in the body of a man with the anointing presence of God. Just think about that for a moment, consider carefully what this could mean to you as a believer today as you walk the Earth as a Man or Woman anointed with the presence of God.

The Final Verdict

Even though we walk as men, in our fleshy bodies, the Anointing of the Holy Spirit is so significant to us that it can even have an effect upon our natural bodies (Romans 8:10). Long life, healing and physical deliverance are all available through the Anointing. We must press in by faith in order to understand this great truth further.

Have you ever noticed that neither the Bible nor any other historically recorded writings bear any record of Jesus ever being sick? Some have suggested that because Luke may have been a Physician, he must have been sick at some point. I disagree entirely with that position. I believe that sickness was an impossibility in the body of Christ, I will explain why in the following paragraphs.

The Blood of Jesus

I want to share one final fact before concluding this chapter. The Bible teaches us that the major result of sin is death. This was the first and only Law of the Garden of Eden. Death existed only as a consequence of sin. Since our Lord Jesus didn't have any Adamic blood, Death was unable to hold him captive.

Another thought that is worth considering is this: When Jesus walked in the Earth, his nature was completely pure because of the absence of that

Adamic sinful blood. If sin was absent then Death must have been absent also. Death had absolutely no relationship with him! In point of fact, Death was dead to him because sin had given it no life. Stop and think about that carefully. Selah!

I believe that had it not have been for the Cross of Calvary, with that Holy anointing on his body, he would have been an immortal human being! I realise that this is not provable, since it is a hypothetical scenario, however it is based on the Word of God and completely justifiable through scripture. I therefore present it only to further glorify the divine and perfect nature of Jesus our Anointed King. Galatians 3:13 tells us that Every Sickness and disease is a curse of the Law. Again, I submit that since Jesus Christ had no relationship with the curse, it was impossible for him to be significantly sick. The more you and I are able to get a grasp of this, the more faith we will receive to fight sin, sickness and the curse in our own lives. Perhaps one day, some of us may even be bold enough to say that if sickness was not possible in the body of Jesus, then by his stripes we really are healed! AND therefore equally sickness has no place in the body of Christ today! Symptoms of sickness will attack us but an individual who is able to receive this revelation by faith can receive glorious healing from it.

Since this is a legal issue, I thought you may like to take a look at the final court records as I imagine them.

Judgement and Sentence

According to I Corinthians 15:57, The believer in Jesus Christ has the victory over satan's authority in his life because the anointing (the Holy Spirit) has been legally placed in his spirit man through faith in God. He is not acting in his own flesh or authority, but in the body and authority of the Lord. Legally speaking, the Devil has no case against him because he acts in the name of another not himself. (Revelation 12:10) The plaintiff therefore must make his representations against him directly to the Judge (God).

According to the book of Romans chapter 8:14 and John 17:12, The Lord Jesus is awarded full and complete legal custody of every believer in the Earth by way of legal adoption. Because they are his sons, all of the usual benefits will apply. They are also legal heirs to the Kingdom of his Father, having right of attorney in the Earth, until the return of the Lord himself.

According to John 14:16, The believer in Christ is also awarded free legal protection in the form of the Holy Spirit. As long as he is acting in the name of the Lord, he shall be exempt from re-trial. Cases of representation of this nature shall be dismissed by the Highest Court of Heaven.

According to the Holy Bible, the believer in Christ has rightful legal authority in this world, because he acts on behalf of he who has been given the total authority. Matthew 28:18 He is permitted, according to the precedent set in Acts 10:37 to go about carrying the anointing freely, doing good, and healing all who are oppressed of the Devil for God is LEGALLY with him.

It is the final judgement of the court of God that the plaintiff must pay the legal costs of this case, but since he is obviously unable to meet such costs, he is sentenced to spend all eternity in the lake of fire.

Case and chapter Closed.

5. The Anti Anointing

The true meaning of the term Anti Christ.

Before I go any further, I want to make the following statement emphatically clear.

I believe in the Holy Trinity, The Father. God. The Son, Jesus. and the third member who is The Holy Ghost.

I felt it necessary to stress this as, the following statement could be challenging to many.

When Jesus came to the Earth, He was not functioning as God, but as a MAN. As we have already seen He referred to himself mainly as the son of man. (MANKIND) In the four Gospels, Jesus refers to himself some eighty four times as the SON OF MAN.

Conversely, satan and demons never referred to him as the son of man but always as the Son of God. Their purpose in doing so was to attempt to identify Jesus as God, thereby accusing the Almighty of sending a God to do the saving of mankind. If this were true, God would be unjust because he had already declared that the Messiah would be the seed of the Woman *(a member of the race of Mankind)*.

In the following scripture, we see a demon attempting to adjure Jesus by his right of legal dominion before God. Adjure is a legal term meaning charge or request (a person) solemnly or earnestly, esp. under oath.

Mark 5:2 *And when He had come out of the boat, immediately there met Him out of the tombs a man with an unclean spirit, (3) who had his dwelling among the tombs; and no one could bind him, not even with chains, (4) because he had often been bound with shackles and chains. And the chains had been pulled apart by him, and the shackles broken in pieces; neither could anyone tame him. (5) And always, night and day, he was in the mountains and in the tombs, crying out and cutting himself with stones.*

6 *When he saw Jesus from afar, he ran and worshipped Him. (7) And he cried out with a loud voice and said, What have I to do with You, Jesus, Son of the Most High God? I implore You by God that You do not torment me.*

8 *For He said to him, Come out of the man, unclean spirit!*

We have all seen the Hollywood representations of the Anti Christ. In the movie The Omen he was depicted as a tremendously powerful business man, who rises into the world of politics to become the ruler of the world. In other movies he is depicted as the caped red horned devil, whilst other writers have depicted him as an all powerful sometimes faceless evil force in the Earth. But if you will, allow the scriptures to present you with a more complete picture of our nemesis. We now understand what the term Christ means so we can go ahead and translate the word Anti Christ accurately. So, this is that Spirit of Anti Christ, which literally means opposed to the message of the anointing.

The Anti Christ spirit maintains that it was not MAN but God himself that came to save mankind, therefore attempting to make God a liar.

In the following scripture the Apostle John gives guidance in recognizing the Spirit of anti CHRIST.

1 John 4:2 *By this you know the Spirit of God: Every spirit that confesses that Jesus Christ has come in the flesh is of God, 3 and every spirit that does not confess that Jesus Christ has come in the flesh is not of God. And this is the spirit of the Antichrist, which you have heard was coming, and is now already in the world.*

Notice the key words: *In the flesh* appearing in both verses.

Jesus came to the Earth functioning as the son of Man but it is only by the revelation of the Holy Spirit that we may know him as the Son of God. When Jesus asked the Disciples "Who do men say that I the son of man am"? He was referring to himself as a member of the race of mankind. Jesus said, that the answer that Peter gave, came directly from God and not from man, so Jesus could not have told them that he was the son of God. That revelation had to have come directly from God.

Some people who misunderstand the above statements will simply say that Jesus is God, and in a very real sense they are not at all wrong. However, it is erroneous to suggest that Jesus came to Earth functioning as God, because if he did, things would have worked out a lot differently. He came as the gentle Lamb of God who takes away the sins of the world. Opening not his mouth but taking the chastisement of all of mankind on his own back.

Is 53:7 *He was oppressed and He was afflicted, Yet He opened not His mouth; He was led as a lamb to the slaughter, And as a sheep before its shearers is silent, So He opened not His mouth..*

There is further evidence that Jesus came functioning as a man and not as God, we can find this in the book of James, chapter 1:13 which says

Let no one say when he is tempted, I am tempted by God; for God cannot be tempted by evil, nor does He Himself tempt anyone.

My conclusion is as follows: God cannot be tempted with evil. And that is the end of it. Now take a look at the following scripture taken from the book of Hebrews:

Hebrews 2:17 *Therefore, in all things He had to be made like His brethren, that He might be a merciful and faithful High Priest in things pertaining to God, to make propitiation for the sins of the people. 18 For in that He Himself has suffered, being tempted, He is able to aid those who are tempted.*

And just in case there was any confusion about this the writer states the same, again in chapter four.

Heb 4:15 *For we do not have a High Priest who cannot sympathize with our weaknesses, but was in all points tempted as we are, yet without sin.*

Now, if Jesus came functioning as God, the two scriptures above, could not be true because, simply put, if Jesus was GOD he could not have been tempted. And since we know that all scripture is true, we must therefore conclude that Jesus came to Earth functioning as a MAN.

He *was* a man, but he said that the "Spirit of the Lord is upon me, because he has anointed me". Jesus didn't go anywhere without his anointing and that's why we call him Jesus CHRIST. It was the anointing which endued the natural body of Jesus with Holy Ghost power and ability, to; open blind eyes, Straighten limbs, Curse fig trees, Change water into wine, Walk on water, Feed five thousand people, Cast out demons and raise the dead, because the anointing IS the Power and the Presence and the Ability of God in MAN. Hallelujah!

Excuse my English but that really gets me going when I think about it. God has all of his power, all of his ability all of his wisdom walking in the Earth in the form of a man and the DEVIL COULDN'T DO ANYTHING ABOUT IT. Jesus was absolutely untouchable, the devil tried to accuse him, tempt him, throw him off of cliffs but nothing doing, Jesus wasn't having any of it, he just said "Oh that devil has nothing in me", and carried on about his business. **BECAUSE HE WAS ANOINTED** glory be to God - Hallelujah.

You can do the same! If you are a real Christian, (anointed one), you are walking with the same presence inside of you that the Lord had inside of him. That Devil has nothing in you because the Lord is in you. You are a victorious, Spirit led, tongue talking, Holy Ghost filled, praising, winning, God loved Son, of the most high God. Though your enemy, the Devil may try to break and destroy you with the trials of this World. You have the Victory through the Anointing who resides on the inside of you. Glory to God! If I could write in tongues, I would write some right here! God is awesome and now you are too! Hallelujah!

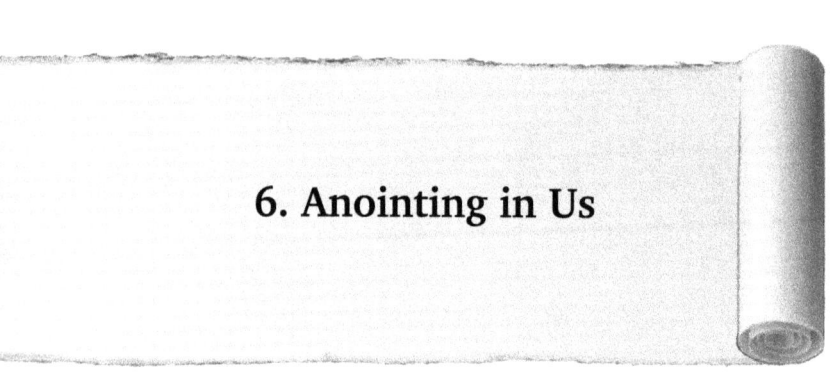

6. Anointing in Us

Sometimes when I am preaching or teaching the Word of God, I can suddenly become aware that I am no longer struggling with my own personal thoughts. It is as if someone is doing the thinking for me. I can hear myself speaking but there is a sensation of literally walking on water as the Word courses through me into the lives of the congregation of believers. I recognize this as the anointing because the Spirit has taken the lead and I am flowing with him. Sometimes during those times, I will do and say things which, under normal circumstances I would be afraid to. A boldness and confidence comes over me that literally flows directly from the heart of God.

I recognize this as the anointing. Often times members of the congregation can see it and comment about the anointing (the presence of the Holy Spirit) on me. Likewise, in our daily lives people recognize the anointing on us, they don't always understand what they see but they see something and usually respond to it either positively or negatively.

At one time in my walk I used to get what I call the crazies. I could be on a train or a bus and every time without fail if there was someone with a drink problem or dual personality issues or to coin a popular phrase completely lunatic, they would always make a beeline for yours truly. Honestly, there could be 100 people in the carriage but they would head straight for me, every time. If this kind of thing happens to you, don't worry, it's probably evidence that like Christ, you also are anointed to help them. Demonic forces are attracted to the anointing in exactly the same way that they were attracted to the Christ. The more that you operate in the things of God the more attention you will attract from the Spirit realm but don't worry, its not all bad. Angels also are attracted and obedient to the presence of God in your life, and that makes for an exciting walk with the Lord.

Demons recognized Jesus from afar, and when they spotted him, it drove them crazy. Running was no good, they had to stay and start talking ugly to Jesus until he would simply cast them out with a few words. Likewise, as the body of Christ, (the anointed), demons and people under their influence will be attracted to you but remember, you have power over them. They may try to confuse, distract, accuse, annoy or even tempt you but always bear in mind, it isn't you they are actually after, it is that anointing on your life.

Each demon that Jesus encountered in those days knew that he was anointed and that he could destroy them at any time. As part of the body of Christ we also have that same power, Hallelujah!

The child of God, therefore, must learn to recognize these antichristic forces and how to use the word and the power of God to cast them out or remove them completely. The Anointed one went about doing good and healing all who are oppressed of the devil. Likewise as CHRISTIANS or anointed ones you are anointed with the Holy Spirit and power to do the same.

How does the Anointing come?

So how did the anointing get in us? This brings me to one of the most fascinating facets of the Earth walk of Jesus which is his birth, If we are to fully understand the anointing and it's purpose, we can grasp some incredible truths from the following accounts.

We go back to the word of God where we see a young virgin girl named Mary being visited by an angel.

26 *Now in the sixth month the angel Gabriel was sent by God to a city of Galilee named Nazareth, (27) to a virgin betrothed to a man whose name was Joseph, of the house of David. The virgin's name was Mary. (28) And having come in, the angel said to her, "Rejoice, highly favoured one, the Lord is with you; blessed are you among women!"*

29 *But when she saw him, she was troubled at his saying, and considered what manner of greeting this was. (30) Then the angel said to her, "Do not be afraid, Mary, for you have found favour with God. (31) And behold, you will conceive in your womb and bring forth a Son, and shall call His name Jesus. (32) He will be great, and will be called the Son of the*

Highest; and the Lord God will give Him the throne of His father David. (33) And He will reign over the house of Jacob forever, and of His kingdom there will be no end."

34 Then Mary said to the angel, "How can this be, since I do not know a man?"

35 And the angel answered and said to her, "The Holy Spirit will come upon you, and the power of the Highest will overshadow you; therefore, also, that Holy One who is to be born will be called the Son of God. (36) Now indeed, Elizabeth your relative has also conceived a son in her old age; and this is now the sixth month for her who was called barren. (37) For with God nothing will be impossible."

38 Then Mary said, "Behold the maidservant of the Lord! Let it be to me according to your word." And the angel departed from her

I have included the entire script because this is such a beautiful scripture, full of revelation and meaning.

I wish to draw your attention to Mary's final statement to the Angel Gabriel. "Behold, the handmaid of the Lord, be it unto me according to your word". Hebrew scholars suggest that the text used here was actually,

"No word spoken by God is without Power".

Wow, looks like Mary is a Woman of revelation! She understood something about the Word of God that will change both hers and our lives forever.

This was the day that God the Father himself had prophesied in the Garden of Eden. This was the seed of the woman that God saw in Eve, but Mary would not be born for generations to come. Mary's faith was the miracle that allowed the baby Jesus to be born. The very second that she said these words to the Lord, something happened. The word that she heard settled in her, it found her faith and mixed with it and they together ignited a spark of divine matter still resident in this daughter of Eve. The divine matter was a human sperm, a holy micro organism of life as the word had become flesh in her womb.

In the first chapter of the book of John, we are clearly shown this progression.

John 1:1 *In the beginning was the Word, and the Word was with God, and the Word was God.*

2 *The same was in the beginning with God.*

3 *All things were made by him; and without him was not any thing made that was made.*

4 *In him was life; and the life was the light of men.*

Here we see Jesus, in his original form. God and his word are one and the same. As we read on we see the following statement:

John 1:14 *And the Word became flesh and dwelt among us, and we beheld His glory, the glory as of the only begotten of the Father, full of grace and truth.*

Two amazing things happened here, Firstly, the word became flesh in Mary's womb and secondly, a spiritual precedent had been patterned for us as believers to be born into the body of Christ through the word.

JESUS IS THE SON OF GOD BORN BY FAITH IN THE WORD OF GOD

WE ARE SONS OF GOD BORN BY FAITH IN THE WORD OF GOD

John 1:12 *But as many as received him, to them gave he power to become the sons of God, even to them that believe on his name:*

13 *Which were born, not of blood, nor of the will of the flesh, nor of the will of man, but of God.*

Earlier we told you that the word glory means to honour. The word glory can also be defined as "to make manifest". Therefore, the glory of the mystery could be defined as the manifestation of the mystery, in other words, it is, how this mystery relates to us. We are to become the sons of God through the word of God IN US. In this, I believe we have found the Glory of the mystery, the word being made manifest in us has through its inherent ability, caused us to become the Sons of God. We have become new creatures through the anointing.

2Cor 5:17 Therefore, if anyone is in Christ, he is a new creation; old things have passed away; behold, all things have become new.

There is much more to say on the subject of Sonship so we will deal with the subject in its entirety later. Before we can fully understand our position as sons, it would behove us to get a better understanding of the power that made us such.

7. Burdens and Yokes

I sat on the edge of my pew in church the day that I first heard this subject the subject of the anointing being preached. It was the first time that I ever heard a definition of the anointing and I was absolutely hooked by it. Every time the preacher used the word anointing, he added the phrase which is the Burden removing yoke destroying power of God, but why? This was a question which plagued me for years following.

Our answer can be found in the tenth chapter of Isaiah, verse 27 New King James version:

27 *It shall come to pass in that day, That his burden will be taken away from your shoulder, And his yoke from your neck, And the yoke will be destroyed because of the anointing oil.*

What is a burden?

Something that you carry which has a tendency to weigh you down.

What is a yoke?

A yoke is a harness that was used mainly by farmers and such-like. It was used to hold two animals together usually by the neck, e.g. carthorses or plough oxen.

Another way of saying "take away" is to remove, so we see that the Anointing is the burden remover.

We can also see that the Anointing is the yoke destroyer, so we could define the Anointing as the:

Burden Removing, Yoke Destroying Power of God

We shouted, screamed and fell out at the wonderful revelation we received during that awesome week of revealing back in 1995, however, my joy was short lived.

As I returned to my home and began to break down, translate and meditate the scriptures one by one as we had been taught to do. I began to feel as though, as awesome as it may have been to us, something was missing from this definition. I didn't know what, but I just knew that something was missing. Over the years I had begun to learn that whenever I would feel that way, it was a prompting from the Holy Spirit to seek him further on a particular subject. I therefore set about seeking the Lord diligently concerning my feeling that something was missing.

Some time later, the answer dawned on me, like the sun rising on the horizon of my life, I suddenly saw the missing piece of the puzzle! You see, the Apostle Paul said that there was a "mystery of Christ", a mystery is not solved by the passing on of a memorable definition, you solve the mystery by the revealing of the Holy Spirit directly to the heart of his children who seek him for it. Consider the following scripture carefully.

Proverbs 25:2 *It is the glory of God to conceal a thing: but the honour of kings is to search out a matter.*

Believe me friend, on this matter I sought him, I cried, wept and slobbered before the Lord diligently for over two years before he revealed the following truths to me. So please don't take lightly what you are about to see, for although you may read it in a matter of minutes, I have paid a considerable price to receive it of the Lord!

As I was studying the Bible in regard to the Anointing, I noticed the following while reading the book of Isaiah.

Isa 61:1 *"The Spirit of the Lord God is upon Me,*

Because the Lord has anointed Me

To preach good tidings to the poor;

He has sent Me to heal the broken-hearted,

To proclaim liberty to the captives,

And the opening of the prison to those who are bound

The Bible said the **Spirit of the Lord** is upon me **BECAUSE** the Lord has anointed me. I continued my study into the book of Luke where again the same scripture was read but this time by the Christ himself.

Luke 4:*16-20 So He came to Nazareth, where He had been brought up. And as His custom was, He went into the synagogue on the Sabbath day, and stood up to read. And He was handed the book of the prophet Isaiah. And when He had opened the book, He found the place where it was written:*

"The Spirit of the Lord is upon Me,

Because He has anointed Me

To preach the gospel to the poor;

He has sent Me to heal the broken-hearted,

To proclaim liberty to the captives

And recovery of sight to the blind,

To set at liberty those who are oppressed;

To proclaim the acceptable year of the Lord."

Then He closed the book, and gave it back to the attendant and sat down. And the eyes of all who were in the synagogue were fixed on Him.

Again, the words just seemed to jump off the page at me.. The Spirit of the Lord is upon me, because he has anointed me!

Again, I continued my study into the book of Acts where I found Peter's account of the anointing

Acts 10 37-38 *that word you know, which was proclaimed throughout all Judea, and began from*

Galilee after the baptism which John preached: how God anointed Jesus of Nazareth with the Holy Spirit and with power, who went about doing good and healing all who were oppressed by the devil, for God was with Him.

The bible says that out of the mouth of two or three witnesses shall the truth be established and this was the establishing witness **"How God anointed Jesus of Nazareth with the Holy Ghost and with power"**…

The burden removing yoke destroying power of God was one of the after effects of the anointing. Notice the phrase **"and with Power"** in other words the power didn't come first, but we see clearly from the three scriptures you have just read **THE HOLY SPIRIT CAME FIRST AND WAS FOLLOWED BY THE POWER!**

Yes, suddenly, the truth was staring me right in the eyes… **The Anointing is the Holy Spirit!** And He brings his POWER with him.

If you need further assurance of this look in Acts

Acts 1:8 *But you shall receive power when the Holy Spirit has come upon you; and you shall be witnesses to Me in Jerusalem, and in all Judea and Samaria, and to the end of the earth."*

Notice when the power came, after, after, after, AFTER, that the Holy Ghost has come upon you. So, is the phrase "the burden removing yoke destroying power of God" incorrect? My answer is no it isn't incorrect, however, it now seems to be incomplete because you cannot walk in the Power of God until the Spirit comes and the Spirit himself is the anointing.

In conclusion of this subject may I offer the following thoughts for you to consider. How many times have you heard the phrase "that was really an anointed song" or "the anointing on this man or woman is really awesome" or perhaps you have even said "I want to have an anointing" like brother or sister so and so.

Consider carefully what is actually being said through these statements because they too are incomplete, not considering the personality of the Holy Spirit who is the true anointing of God in our lives, giving us ability beyond our own natural ability to do incredible, seemingly impossible, above the natural things.

As an illustration, some time ago, I served as a Pastor under a church organisation which was presided over by a certain Bishop who would regularly attend our branch of the church. During one particular service, I heard him remarking that he had noticed that the anointing on my life had increased since I had begun to serve within his particular organisation.

He further commented that in his opinion, as long as I remained a part of that particular organisation the anointing would continue to grow implying that if I ever chose to leave, that the anointing would not be so evident on my life.

This was an understandable but extremely erroneous statement to me. It was understandable because I knew that this minister, although he operated in great anointing power, had not sought the Lord as I had concerning the source of the anointing, and therefore he made the statement based on his understanding of what the anointing was. He was a great man of God whom I respected very much so It wasn't so much that he was incorrect but that his understanding of the anointing was incomplete.

The truth, in fact, was that the church organisation, the Anointing and the power of God all belong to God and not to any man. The truth in fact, is that the power of God had, at that time begun to operate marvellously in my personal ministry because God had desired for it to be so because the church was filled with believers who needed a true manifestation of God in their lives. I was both willing and available and therefore used as a vessel of the Lords favour.

The truth was that as long as there are yokes to be destroyed and burdens to be removed, God himself WILL anoint ANYONE whose heart is perfect towards him to be the person though whom he will administer his favour and grace towards mankind.

The anointing is not subject to any man but to God and God alone. I consequently left that organisation with great confidence, being led of the Holy Ghost to do so, and you will be happy to hear, the anointing increased steadily as I drew closer to God in my personal walk and ministry.

Don't let people frighten you into believing that the anointing of God is subject to any man, your faith must be in God and God alone, if you are to walk in the true anointing.

# 8. Defining the Anointing

We know that God has given us authority over demonic powers through the anointing. As wonderful as this truth is or may sound, we will never truly walk in the revelation of this fact until we are able to identify exactly what the anointing truly is. The real question is: How do we define the Anointing? A definition allows us to receive the ultimate clarity about a thing because it gives us the complete understanding in as it were, a nutshell.

Historically, which is of course Biblically speaking, there have only ever been two forms of the Anointing in the Earth. We can define them as

The Pre-cross Anointing and 2. The Post-cross Anointing. I believe that one Biblical reference for these two states of Anointing can be found in the book of Hosea which says in chapter:

3 *Let us know, Let us pursue the knowledge of the Lord. His going forth is established as the morning; He will come to us like the rain,*

Like the latter and former rain to the earth.

I believe the moment that defines the difference between the two states is the moment when the Lord Jesus went to the Cross of Calvary. I believe that he carried the final instalment of the former rain and gave birth to the new and latter rain which would fall forever in the Earth until the time of its restoration.

When Jesus walked the Earth, he received the Anointing from God **ON HIM**. (Luke 4:18 and Isaiah 61:1) This was the only way that the Anointing could be present in the Earth before Jesus made that ultimate sacrifice on the cross of Calvary. We also can find evidence of others who walked in the anointing before Jesus. Examples include: Elijah, Elisha, David, Aaron, Samson Samuel and others. The anointing showed up ON all of these men at some point in their individual ministries, indeed, in the case of Aaron, the anointing on his body must have been so strong that even after he died, the rod which he would hold in his hand was still filled with life giving anointing power which caused it to bud! See Heb 9:4.

Another example is Samson who was anointed with extraordinary strength, The Bible states in the Book of Judges:

Jdg 13:24 *So the woman bore a son and called his name Samson; and the child grew, and the Lord blessed him.*

25 *And the Spirit of the Lord began to move upon him at Mahaneh Dan between Zorah and Eshtaol.*

The blessing of the Lord was upon him, the Spirit of the Lord was also upon him and later in his life we read the following account when Samson ripped a lion in two with his bare hands:

Judges 14:6 *And the Spirit of the Lord came mightily upon him, and he tore the lion apart as one would have torn apart a young goat, though he had nothing in his hand. But he did not tell his father or his mother what he had done.*

We have defined the Spirit of the Lord as the Anointing so now we can say that it was the Anointing of God which came upon the Young Samson. The result of this was that he had incredible Burden removing yoke destroying power on his life. This power enabled Samson to overcome a strong young lion as if it were nothing at all. Hallelujah!

Samson's strength came from the anointing of God ON HIM. This was the former rain of God's presence which, as mighty as it was, only served only as a template for the greater presence of God which was to follow the supreme sacrifice of Jesus Christ, the Son of Man, which was to qualify all of mankind for the latter rain anointing.

THIS ANOINTING WOULD NOT ONLY BE ON MAN,

THIS ANOINTING IS INSIDE AND ON MAN.

The Riches of the Glory of the Mystery of Christ

Are you ready to receive the Riches of the Glory of the Mystery of Christ? Firstly let us pay close attention to some key words which the Lord spoke in the book of John, just before he went to the cross of Calvary.

John 14:15 *If you love Me, keep My commandments.*

16 *And I will pray the Father, and He will give you another Helper, that He may abide with you forever; the Spirit of truth, whom the world cannot receive, because it neither sees Him nor knows Him; but you know Him, for He dwells with you and will be in you.*

You see, the Lord Jesus told us where this new Anointing would abide, IN us IN the believer! IN me and IN you! Just imagine for a second what that anointing might be in you to do! You are a world changing, anointed child of God, pregnant with God's ability inside you. His ability is ready willing and able to eradicate every hindrance to your blessing and Joy in the name of Jesus.

Now let us re-consider the words of the Apostle Paul which we discussed in the first chapter of this book. In the 1st Chapter of Colossians the word "mystery" occurs. As I told you at the beginning of this book, when you see the word mystery, it means that there is an enigma. Meaning something is hidden from obvious view.

26 *Even the **mystery** which hath been hid from ages and from generations, but now is made manifest to his saints.*

27 *To whom God would make known what is the riches of the glory of this mystery among the Gentiles;* **which is Christ in you***, the hope of glory.*

We have got to get some thing settled before we go any further. The Apostle Paul made the above statement crystal clear for us. He said that the Riches of the Glory of the Mystery of CHRIST, is **CHRIST IN YOU**. Now if we translate this, he is simply saying that it is the anointing in you which is your hope of glory. Please hear my heart carefully, I am not trying to despiritualise the word Christ, or to take the focus away from his obvious deity. My intention is to lift up the son of man to his place of power and glory in our lives. Listen, Jesus didn't just come to prepare a place for us in Heaven. He came also to destroy the works of the devil and to give us real POWER over all of the power of the enemy. Now if we are going to get a revelation of Christ in us, we are going to have to see it in the word first because faith comes by hearing and hearing by the word.

If I can show you clearly, by the word of God, that you are anointed, then you in turn will be able to seek out the riches for yourself. I can't get your riches for you. I am still too busy trying to get my own. It's like the old saying, you can take the horse to the water but you can't make it drink. You have to desire this anointing on your life, take a good old gulp of that water and let it begin to bring life to you.

8. Defining the Anointing

Read the following scriptures out loud:

2 Cor 1:21 *Now He who establishes us with you in Christ and has anointed us is God,*

Notice, God HAS, (past tense) anointed US, can you see it? God has established us and anointed us. If you have really grasped that, you will be able to say this with real passion and faith.

"THROUGH JESUS, I HAVE BECOME THE ANOINTED.

"THE ANOINTER GOD, HAS ANOINTED ME WITH THE ANOINTING... WHO IS THE HOLY SPIRIT".

"I AM, THEREFORE, ANOINTED."

Now read the following again out loud.

1 John 2:26 *These things I have written to you concerning those who try to deceive you. 27 But the anointing which you have received from Him abides in you, and you do not need that anyone teach you; but as the same anointing teaches you concerning all things, and is true, and is not a lie, and just as it has taught you, you will abide in Him.*

Notice, once again, the anointing which you **have received** (past tense) abides IN US. Christ is in us and that is our hope of glory, remember always translate and meditate. These scriptures are the doorway to the miraculous power and presence of

God in our lives, translate and meditate them until you have it settled in your own heart.

The degree of the manifestation of the anointing in our lives will always be proportionately related to the degree with which we are settled on the fact that we are anointed. Now you understand what the anointing is, translate and meditate, translate and mediate. In fact, anywhere you see the word Christ, translate and meditate until the revelation becomes clear to you. The presence of Christ means presence of God through the Holy Spirit in you, the hope of glory.

It is our love for the Lord Jesus, the Father and the Holy Spirit which produces an obedient walk. That obedience produces the anointing in our lives.

Practically every word that Jesus spoke involved the anointing in some way or form. In fact, with some meditation you can deduce that it was the only subject he ever preached. He hardly ever spoke about anything else because this was why he was sent, to bring the Word of the anointing to us. One of my favourite verses of scripture in the Holy Bible is this one: We have seen it before but let's revisit it now.

2 Cor 5:17 *Therefore, if anyone is in Christ, he is a new creation; old things have passed away; behold, all things have become new.*

And all things are of God, who hath reconciled us to himself by Jesus Christ, and hath given to us the ministry of reconciliation;

To wit, that God was in Christ, reconciling the world unto himself, not imputing their trespasses unto them; and hath committed unto us the word of reconciliation.

This is absolutely, beyond a doubt, one the most profound verses of scripture to me. Verse 19 says God Was in CHRIST. Allow me to translate this for us. Here are three Clear facts about the anointing that we see through this scripture.

God was and is in the Anointing process

GOD is in the Holy Spirit

Which means that GOD is in you

It was the Fathers desire that we should be anointed like Jesus and his disciples like Peter and Paul. God has never said that the anointing would weaken with every generation that passes. Jesus didn't say that either but rather, he said that we would do greater things than he did, because he is going to be with, the Father. (John 14:12) It seems that, over time, the message was lost, and consequently, the church, has weakened. We are not nearly as powerful as we should be, and I believe we will never be, until believers once again begin to make the glad and confident confession which we have just read out loud. "I AM ANOINTED". There is absolutely no doubt in my mind at all that Jesus wants us to know we are anointed. The time has come for this word to return to the church, it is time for it to be back in the mouths of believers, ready to take this world back and live in the God designed authority that is our heritage in this anointing. Hallelujah!

It is time for the devils which have ruled this planet since the time of Adam, to tremble at the notion of millions of anointed brothers and sisters in Christ declaring through faith and prayer that they are anointed to remove all of the power of the enemy from this planet, to the glory to God the anointer..

Please Get the following sentence in your Spirit, it comes directly from the throne room of God the father.

GOD IS IN YOU. HE IS PART OF YOU THROUGH THE ANOINTING, YOU ARE PART OF HIM THROUGH CHRIST!

Hallelujah!

You know I am convinced that many of us do not walk in the maximum presence of God, primarily because we do not ask for it and subsequently, we don't receive it by faith. If you have been challenged by the words of this book thus far perhaps it is time for you to ask God in faith, for the anointing? Consider the following scripture taken from the book of Luke.

Luke 11:11-13 *If a son asks for bread from any father among you, will he give him a stone? Or if he asks for a fish, will he give him a serpent instead of a fish? Or if he asks for an egg, will he offer him a scorpion?*

If you then, being evil, know how to give good gifts to your children, how much more will your heavenly Father give the Holy Spirit to those who ask Him.

We can now define the **Anointing** as the Presence of the Holy Spirit in our Hearts, based on the scripture which we read in Acts 10:37 "How God anointed Jesus of Nazareth with the Holy Spirit and Power". We can also define the Power as that which accompanies the Holy Spirit, allowing him to do good and heal all who were oppressed of the Devil.

Take a moment right now to ask your father for his anointing in and on your life. He will not refuse you, and that is the BIBLE TRUTH.

Pray this prayer right now:

Dear Heavenly Father,

I accept your great and wonderful sacrifice on the cross of Calvary. Lord Jesus I thank you for dying for my sins and cleansing me by your blood which is most precious.

Father, I am now your child and you said in your word that if I ask you, that you will give me the Holy Spirit to dwell with me forever. I ask you now, in the name of Jesus to give me the Holy Spirit and I thank you, for I ask this now in Jesus name.

Stop for just a moment and consider these words carefully. The anointing, by now, should not be a mystery to you any more. The term anointing should mean much more than a religious notion or magical mystical power. The presence of God in your life will do astounding things for you. As another writer said, it is God putting his Super on your Natural, giving you SUPERNATURAL power! As we grow in Christ, we are literally growing in the anointing, growing in the presence of God. As we translate and meditate upon this subject, miracles become more and more prevalent and commonplace in our lives, until eventually, we are walking continuously in the miraculous presence of God.

The anointing of God on your life comes not only for the sake of others, in fact its primary purpose to you, is to help you. The presence of God will change you, give you favour with men, with work colleagues, at school etc. The presence of God will give you wisdom, protect and even heal you, and I hope to prove that to you in the following chapters.

9. The Healing Anointing

At this point in the book, I want to show you by personal and practical experience, just why understanding this anointing is so important to us as believers. Remember the instruction that the Lord gave us from the book of Matthew, chapter thirteen, "He that receives the seed into the good soil is the one who hears the Word and understands it! He will bring forth the fruit of it, some thirty, sixty and one hundred fold". I pray that you will be one who will bring forth 100 fold on this revelation of Christ, and that through it you shall receive your total healing in Jesus name.

I want to regale with you this true account of a healing which I received divinely through the knowledge of the Anointing. This account is most precious to me. It is true and accurate and carries the anointing presence every time I share it. I have been blessed to receive all manner of healings through the Lord's anointed presence in my life. They were all glorious at the time, however, this particular healing left a powerful mark on me forever.

Throughout my life as a believer I have made a number of errors. I made mistakes with relationships, business, and sometimes in ministry. I made such a mistake in 2006, the resulting effects of which were completely catastrophic to me and my family. You see I had attempted to start a ministry which, in the end, I did not possess the faith to continue with. My mistake cost me almost everything. It cost me my reputation, my business and our home, which finally had to be sold in order to cover the financial effects of my failure. Inevitably and finally, my health began to deteriorate rapidly.

I began to suffer with chronic tiredness, a condition that results from a number of ailments, most of them serious. I prayed and prayed and received some relief but ultimately, the condition only seemed to worsen. I visited the Doctor and described my symptoms, which by now had increased in both number and severity. I had debilitating pain in different parts of my body. A consistently horrible nausea which accompanied an indescribable tiredness. The best way I can describe it is that it felt as though I was close to death.

Feeling absolutely desperate, I began to give attention to God's Word, the Holy Bible. I remembered the scripture which said that his word was health and healing to my flesh.

Proverbs 4:22 *For they are life to those who find them, And health to all their flesh.*

I began to read from the pen of one of my favourite authors, Charles Capps, the book was called Faith and Confession. The Word of God through him began to transform my thinking. I understood that healing could be mine through the confession of the Word of God by faith. Faith began to rise up in me and I began to believe that I could be healed from the dastardly attack, if I could just find the right words to confess from the Word of God.

I don't remember which part of the book did it. Mr Capp's words are like missiles striking at unbelief and poor teaching, knocking down old sacred cows and building your faith, precept upon precept, line upon line. It's like feasting on a home cooked meal, in which all of the components are cooked just right. Just the way you like it! You take a piece of bread, a piece of Chicken, some macaroni pie and gravy and salad and just get dug in! That's exactly what I was doing, morning, noon and night. Digging in on the Word of God.

As I studied His word, I began to feel somewhat better but a battle began to ensue. It seemed that I would feel better for a short time but then the sickness would return and this time more painfully and with much more debilitating effect.

After some weeks, I was hit with the worst attack ever. I feared the worst as the tiredness seemed to be increasing. I was so tired that I couldn't even sleep. One evening, I was laid on my front room floor because I didn't have the strength to do anything else. A real deep and penetrating fear suddenly came over me. I was so tired that I feared that I would die from this thing. I have always been quite an emotional person, and I thought to myself I better get upstairs to the bedroom where my wife was sleeping, after all, if I am going to die, at least let me be with someone I love and who loves me.

I was so battle weary, I was ready to give up the ghost in defeat, but as I crawled up the stairs of our home, I heard the Lord speaking inside of me. He said "You shall not die, but LIVE". By this time I was a pitiful sight, a grown man, crying on the floor of my bedroom beside my bed because I did not have the strength to get into it.

My loving wife Seva held out her hand to me and began to pray quietly. I didn't want her to know how bad I was feeling and at the same time, somewhere in the back of my mind I remembered what the Lord had said. I said to Seva, that If I could just find the right Words to pray, I am sure I will be healed but I just don't know what to pray or say. I feel awful and I need a word that will give me strength. Seva, now half asleep, paused for a moment and then spoke the following words to me.

"The Lord is your Strength and your Shield".

I replied, what did you say? She repeated the words "the Lord is your strength and your shield...

Now I was vaguely familiar with these words. I knew they were scriptural, but they had never meant anything more than the words of a good Christian Psalm to me. When Seva spoke them that night, I heard the thing very differently. I heard life in those words. I heard my ticket to freedom from this evil disease that I was being gripped by. I said, The Lord is My strength, The Lord is My strength, The Lord is My strength, The Lord is My strength!

As I spoke these words, my mind seemed to argue with me. If the Lord is your strength, why are you so weak? A war literally broke out within me! It was a battle between my Spirit and My Mind!

Then a thought came from deep within me. It was the Voice of God! He said, I am in you, through the Anointing.

My years of studying the anointing were about to suddenly and miraculously produce incredible fruit in my life. You see, I KNEW as a certain FACT that the Lord had made his dwelling in me through CHRIST (The Anointing). I also knew that the scripture could not lie. When my wife said the Lord is your strength, there was an undeniable connection made between my spirit and my mind. Finally, I made the following deduction. The Lord is in me and the Lord is my strength, the Lord is in me and the Lord is my strength...

"If the Lord is my Strength and the Lord is in me, then I have all of the strength I need".

I stopped weeping and wailing instantly and spoke the following words out loud "The Lord is in me, strength is in me"! Before I knew what happened I was standing, then leaping and running around the room, Hallelujah! I had been healed by the presence of God in me. The years of anointing study had finally paid off! I was healed through the presence of God in me. I never suffered that sickness again as I have been walking in the strength of the Lord ever since this time. I was delivered by the Word of his Power. This awakened a tremendous time of revelation and healing in our personal lives and ministry.

The anointing is in your life for a divine purpose! Its mandate is to give you complete victory over every circumstance in your life by faith!

Scripture tells us that we should allow the Word to dwell in us Richly! Let this deep revelation of Christ dwell in you richly!

The origin of the sickness

Some time later, the Lord began to minister to me concerning the origin of the sickness that I passed through at that time. I discovered that its source was definitely satanic. I was hated of the devil because of the good works that I was doing for the Kingdom of God.

Curses and such like work by using words negatively against an individual that evil people wish harm to come to. I don't know exactly who or what was uttered against me but the Lord revealed this in a dream to me. I knew that curses had been spoken BUT the Word of God is more powerful than any curse that may have been uttered against you. Deliverance is available through the anointing! The presence of God within you is greater than any other presence that may try to gain entrance illegally. Greater is he who is in you than he that is in the World.

At this point let me encourage you. Have you been waiting for God to deliver you for a long time? Has sickness, disease, poverty, depression or pain been your burden? Are you yoked to a situation, a curse or a feeling of guilt that has held you bound?

Sometimes the trials that we face seem so hard to bear, it seems that the devil knows and understands the power of the word of Christ in us and battles against us using all of his devices to remove us from our position of faith and power. Sometimes we may even feel like giving up, that our years of pursuing the Lord and His word have been years spent in vain as nothing seems to shift this evil trial that is to try us.

The book of Peter speaks about the fiery trial of our faith, (1 Peter 4:12) it doesn't say it's going to be an easy trial or a simple puzzle or enigma for you to work out, it says it's going to be a fiery trial of your faith. If the anointing is all that God's word says it is, then it is a force that is worth fighting for. Be encouraged right now. Continue to fight the good fight of faith. Continue confessing the word of God, believing, holding onto and adhering to His Word.

In the end, it will produce a harvest of faith in your life.

Before the first and second world wars, Europe lived in a state of peace until evil dictators invaded neighbouring lands with the threat of oppression. Nobody wanted to go to war, nobody wanted to see their children lost in battles, no husband wanted to leave his wife or family, but the threat absolutely would not go away unless they did so. The incredible thing about those times is that men and women found within themselves a courage that they didn't know was there. In fact, they may never have known this power within, had there not been a war and the threat of oppression.

Likewise believer, there is a power in you, a courage, and a boldness. A victory was birthed in you from the moment you received Christ and His anointing on your life. It sits right now, resident in you, waiting upon the impending threat of a dictator, the enemy of your soul. It is available to you right now to remove every burden and every stronghold that you are facing in your life. It will enable you to shout hallelujah, not just with expectant faith but because you have received your victory through Christ.

When we formed the House of Victory in Wellingborough, we sought the Lord for a foundational scripture, He took me to the book of 1 Corinthians 15:57 where it says "But thanks be to

God, which gives us the victory through our Lord and Saviour Jesus Christ the Anointed". Notice the word "which", this is an important word because the word "which" doesn't appear to be referring to the person of Christ, but I believe it points to the true cause of our victory, which is to give thanks to the Lord for the anointing that His son Jesus Christ has made available for us.

In Christ

After I received this miracle, I received a renewed excitement for studying the presence of God in me. I realised that the Holy Spirit had shown me the way to receive victory in every area of my life. Whilst I was on my bedroom floor, I deduced that since Christ was in me, I had all the strength that I would need.

Subsequently, I began to think, "If Christ brought me strength through His presence in me, what else was lying dormant in me that I had not yet realised"? Is there a financial miracle in me? Is there peace in me? Is there joy in me? Is there a new life in me? Are the purposes and plans of God in me?

As I studied these areas one by one, I came to the conclusion that the answer to them all is yes and amen. If Christ is in me, through the presence of the Holy Spirit, I have the answer to every trial waiting to come forth.

Before closing this chapter I would like to leave the following thought with you, Faith isn't faith until you receive it, conceive it, believe it, confess it and see it. The pathway to perfect faith is to recognise the perfect one living on the inside of you. If you can do this, the struggle will be over because faith itself comes from the knowledge of His divine presence. In perfect theological terms, God is the Spirit of faith. With this in mind let's heed the instruction which the Lord left us in Mark 11:23-24.

For assuredly, I say to you, whoever says to this mountain, Be removed and be cast into the sea, and does not doubt in his heart, but believes that those things he says will be done, he will have whatever he says. Therefore I say to you, whatever things you ask when you pray, believe that you receive them, and you will have them.

Here our Lord Jesus shows us both the principle and instruction for faith. Study this diligently until the scripture becomes life in you. Study every word and its meaning until you completely understand both the principle and the instruction.

Notice; Nothing happens by faith until you say it, you can have great faith in your heart, but unless that faith is released through the vessel of words, though the victory is in you, it cannot be made manifest.

God made the worlds by His word. If He had just thought or believed the worlds, they would never have come into existence. It was by the spoken word that He established all things, likewise our faith can only be established by the spoken word. I have faith in the fact that these words will have helped you. After all, God is no respecter of persons, therefore, what He did for me He will do for you by and through His anointing on your life, Amen.

Healing Prayers

As a pastor, I spend very much of my time praying for various illnesses to be healed by God. This was the way in which I came to know him as my saviour, and so I am happy to pray for any need that arises, equally because it boosts my personal faith when people receive this way.

Many times, when I perceive that a person needs an intense prayer or in times when a sickness has reached a very debilitating effect, I turn to the pages of the book of Exodus, Chapter 23 verse 25 which says

And you shall serve the Lord your God and he will bless your bread and your water, and I will take sickness out of the midst of thee.

I get the person to take an ordinary bottle of water and pray these words in faith until they can see it as real, then drink it! Time after time, we have had tremendous results with this scripture but why? Because of the anointing, Hallelujah! Did you see it?

Let me show it to you, notice the three parties involved in the process of healing were as follows:

You (1) will serve the Lord

The Lord (2) will bless your bread and water

And I (3) will take sickness away

Question: Who is the "I" being referred to here? Since the writer had already mentioned God, we must presume that the I referred to here is another entity, and so it is, the third personality of the Holy Trinity, which we have come to know as the Holy Spirit or the Anointing. Now we must always look for these nuggets of faith in the Word of God, once you begin to grasp the revelation, they will just begin to pop up all over the book. Always look for the confirmation of revelations received also, for instance in this case of the healing waters, it is confirmed by this verse taken from proverbs:

Pro 18:14 *The spirit of a man will sustain him in sickness, But who can bear a broken spirit?*

So then, it is the Spirit (Anointing) that provides the healing for the body when we need it. If you are sick right now, why not go and get yourself a glass of God's miracle water?

You put faith in Chemists, Drug Stores, Doctors, Nurses and Physicians! Why not put your faith in the greatest of the great physicians, and in his marvellous, mysterious liquid that we call water?

God is able to transform that fluid into the very healing medicine you need. You can receive your healing by faith in the Word. As you drink, think in terms of the anointing, see the Spirit of God on the face of the water and drink in your miracle. Hallelujah!

Get a bottle and stick a label on it that says God's miracle water, fill it with plain old tap water, claim it as yours and then begin your prayer. I pray that you will soon be hopping and skipping around by the grace of the Lord Jesus Christ. Take a moment to reflect on that before we move on.

10. Living with the Anointing

Col 3:16 *Let the word of Christ dwell in you richly in all wisdom, teaching and admonishing one another in psalms and hymns and spiritual songs, singing with grace in your hearts to the Lord.*

You see, according to this word, we are not just to memorise scripture, (although this may help us somewhat), the true benefit comes from letting or allowing the word dwell in us RICHLY! We have to think and dream and talk and meditate on the anointing, keeping it on our minds and hearts all the time. If you don't want to let your guard down, always keep the anointing on your mind it will deliver you from failure and poverty in Jesus name. Another witness is found in the book of Joshua which teaches us that we should keep the Word on our hearts at all time.

Joshua 1:8 *This Book of the Law shall not depart from your mouth, but you shall meditate in it day and night, that you may observe to do according to all that is written in it. For then you will make your way prosperous, and then you will have good success.*

You see, prosperity is in the anointing, success is in the anointing. If we can keep the anointing on our minds it will make a difference in our lives.

Another scripture says "As a man thinks in his heart, so is he". (Proverbs 23:7) In other words, what you mediate on in your heart will make a huge difference resulting in what will manifest in your life.

Jesus taught us concerning His word also that we should allow the anointing to dwell in us. Dwell means to live, not just to have a place of residence but to let it LIVE in you. In other words, His words should be kept ALIVE IN US AT ALL TIMES! Hallelujah. He said:

John 15:7 *If you abide in Me, and My words abide in you, you will ask what you desire, and it shall be done for you.*

8 By this My Father is glorified, that you bear much fruit; so you will be My disciples.

Apparently, Jesus was saying that if you will allow the word to dwell in you, the result would be that you will have ability to speak to circumstances and have them changed by the Word of his indwelling power. We can also translate this as "You will have ability to request what you delight in and it will be given to you". Glory to God!

So what Word is it that we should let dwell richly and abide in us?

The answer is, the Word of God or the Bible which is God's Holy Word, however, there may be another level of glory waiting for us, if we would dare to delve deeper into this thought! Let's go back into the book of Acts again.

Act 10:37 *that word you know, which was proclaimed throughout all Judea, and began from Galilee after the baptism which John preached:*

38 *How God anointed Jesus of Nazareth with the Holy Spirit and with power, who went about doing good and healing all who were oppressed by the devil, for God was with Him.*

Can you see it? Here in the book of Acts we are being directed to a specific message recorded in our Bibles today. There was no such thing as the New Testament or the King James version back then!

It was the letters being written by Apostle Paul and Peter and other disciples that formed the basis of the New Testament. They were writing the word, under the influence of the Holy Spirit. Those Apostles had Hebraic teachings from the Torah and the Jewish Law which formed the basis of their message but after the cross, they Preached the Word about the Anointing! Christ, The Messiah. It's the word about the Anointing! Once you get a revelation of it, it just seems to keep cropping up. The more you study, translate and meditate upon this revelation, the more you will begin to see it clearly.

When the Apostle Peter preached the Word, the Bible records that the Holy Spirit fell on all who heard it. Peter preached and lived Isaiah 61:1 and the result was, that the people who heard, were anointed by the Word.

But you may say, "How does that relate to me"? "YOU ARE A CHRISTIAN"! Which means, "You are anointed" with the Holy Ghost and with power. You can go about, do good and heal those oppressed of the devil!

Yes, you are anointed to destroy the works of the devil too. We must rise up and let faith take a hold of the message of Christ then walk in it.

One of the things I hear a lot of these days, is the subject of spiritual warfare. Whilst I don't disagree with it, I am challenged by the way some teach it, I have noticed that they almost seem to elevate and empower satan and his minions of demonic forces until we begin to see him as the mighty devil, with power to destroy us.

However, according to the following scripture, Demons (Disembodied evil Spirits) are unable to stand the presence of God, because it torments them.

Mar 5:7 And he cried out with a loud voice and said, What have I to do with You, Jesus, Son of the Most High God? I implore You by God that You do not torment me.

Here we see a demon actually trying to use the authority of God to stop Jesus from tormenting him. He was so desperate to get this torment out of his life that he attempted to use the Word of God himself against our Lord. That's real desperation! The demon was trying to say that it was illegal for God to send another God in the Earth. The presence of God in the Earth torments them. They know that eventually they must end up in a place of torment but not now, not in the Earth. This is a place where they can find maximum effectiveness because here in the Earth, they can find many bodies who are willing to give them a place of domicile.

By bodies, I mean willing human beings who allow demons of sin wilfully into their own lives. Equally demons can enter in through fear, or through prolonged sickness, offence and or curses. BUT the presence of God in the Earth torments them.

Consequently, I believe that the very presence of God in you will torment any demonic force that comes to invade your life. You won't have to do anything except receive the Lord Jesus in your heart and that is it. By faith, the demons of oppression will be tormented by His presence! I believe this by faith! I know that in reality, things may not seem that simple but it will be our faith that will bring us to a new reality of God's presence in our lives.

People are always telling me that I am wrong, and that deliverance is a process which takes time and even though my mind agrees with what they say, being presented with sufficient evidence to hold the theory up, somehow my heart is completely disappointed with this theology. Now, if you are of this mindset, I certainly do not wish to offend you but no matter how I try, I just can't remember the Lord Jesus teaching that way anywhere in scripture. In fact, when I think of Jesus and the Anointing on Him as He walked the Earth, I see multiple demonic forces being instantly cast out. There were no negotiations with the anointing. It was very simple, if you are a burden, you will be removed. If you are yoked to something demonic, the yoke shall be destroyed. Period! I think the only reason why these things are not being manifest in the body of Christ today, is because we lack the faith to see them happen. We are settling for a process, rather than believing for the power. We embrace theologies that explain our inefficiencies rather than seek the perfection that is in Christ.

Say these words out loud, regularly:

"I have the presence of the Lord in me, so every demon will have to flee."

Let that word dwell in you richly! Think on it, meditate on it and speak it until it transfers life into your situation. Every oppressive demon MUST leave you in the name of Jesus, because you are an anointed Son of God, a Christian armed with the presence of God.

11. The Presence of God

The word blessed or blessing occurs some 287 times throughout scripture, the subject is therefore too vast to cover in this book. Suffice to say that the Anointed presence of God brings blessings. You can begin to see this principle clearly in the historical and Biblical accounts of the Ark of the Covenant. This box, overlaid with Gold, and designed according to specific blueprints supplied directly from God was constructed solely for the purpose of carrying the presence of God. Apparently no-one knows exactly what happened to the Ark or where it finally ended up.

I'm pretty sure God knows though. For us, it is a modern day mystery, picked up by Hollywood producers in movies like Raiders of the Lost Ark and others. To the Christian believer, the Ark is not a mystery, but a source of great encouragement and blessing. It represents the presence of God in the Earth, given to the children of His covenant to give them advantage over their enemies and special favour and provision with God.

THIS IS ALSO A PERFECT DEFINITION OF THE ANOINTING! We have the same presence of God, we are engrafted into the same covenant. We have the same blessings, the same advantage, favour and provision! Hallelujah.

Ephesians 2 states:

Eph 2:11 *Therefore remember that you, once Gentiles in the flesh-who are called Uncircumcision by what is called the Circumcision made in the flesh by hands.*

Eph 2:12 *That at that time you were without Christ, being aliens from*

the commonwealth of Israel and strangers from the covenants of promise, having no hope and without God in the world.

13 *But now in Christ Jesus you who once were far off have been brought near by the blood of Christ.*

14 *For He Himself is our peace, who has made both one, and has broken down the middle wall of separation,*

15 *Having abolished in His flesh the enmity, that is, the law of commandments contained in ordinances, so as to create in Himself one new man from the two, thus making peace.*

16 *And that He might reconcile them both to God in one body through the cross, thereby putting to death the enmity.*

17 *And He came and preached peace to you who were afar off and to those who were near.*

18 *For through Him we both have access by one Spirit to the Father.*

19 *Now, therefore, you are no longer strangers and foreigners, but fellow citizens with the saints and members of the household of God,*

20 *having been built on the foundation of the apostles and prophets, Jesus Christ Himself being the chief corner stone,*

21 *in whom the whole building, being fitted together, grows into a holy temple in the Lord,*

22 *in whom you also are being built together for a dwelling place of God in the Spirit. Now therefore ye are no more strangers and foreigners, but fellow citizens with the saints, and of the household of God*

You see we are engrafted into all of the blessings given to the children of Israel through the presence of Jesus Christ in our lives and through His precious blood. All of this is made available to us through the anointing.

The Children of Israel saw miraculous provision through the presence of the Ark of the covenant because it housed the very presence of God, its Biblical record forms the most awesome account of His presence in the Earth, from which, we may now draw some incredible revelation for our walk in the Spirit today.

Beginning in the book of 1 Samuel Chapter 4, we find the complete account of the passage of the Ark into the hands of the Philistine armies, who defeated Israel and laid claim to it. They immediately took the Ark to their own place of worship, the temple of daigon, who was their false God. Here we see the complete account of what happened but let's pick out some highly relevant elements to our topic today.

1 Sam 4:5 *And when the ark of the covenant of the Lord came into the camp, all Israel shouted so loudly that the earth shook.*

Here we see the birth of the prophetic shout! Israel knew and understood the significance of the presence of God; it was a revelation to each and every one of them. This presence was so momentous to them that it caused them to shout with a great shout, not an ordinary shout. This shout actually caused the Earth to RING! The Hebrew word for ring is HUM and it means to agitate or move. Israel's prophetic shout caused the very Earth to rumble! I believe that if the people of God today will seek God for a perfect revelation of his presence, it will cause a shout so mighty that the very Earth around them will be affected by the magnitude of it. Every negative circumstance in our lives will be affected by it and the enemies of our souls will be confused and afraid of it. Stop and meditate on this thought for a moment before moving on. Picture the whole of Israel, shouting with a mighty shout of joy and triumph. The presence of God is with us. The presence of God is with us! Everything around them is electrified by that awesome sound. I believe there is a new sound of worship in the Earth today, which echoes this shout. It is a corporate shout, a prophetic shout. An awesome mixture of human voices and heavenly shofar's reaching from planet Earth to heaven itself changing the world we live in for evermore! Hallelujah!

Look at the result if Israel's great and mighty shout. (1 Sam 4:6-8)

Now when the Philistines heard the noise of the shout, they said, What does the sound of this great shout in the camp of the Hebrews mean? Then they understood that the ark of the Lord had come into the camp.

So the Philistines were afraid, for they said, God has come into the camp! And they said, Woe to us! For such a thing has never happened before.

Woe to us! Who will deliver us from the hand of these mighty Gods? These are the Gods who struck the Egyptians with all the plagues in the wilderness.

Here we see that the Philistines, who now represent the presence of demonic forces, instantly recognise the prophetic shout as the shout of mighty Gods. This is how the anointing should affect every demonic force in our lives as believers. We should be to them as Gods, able to cast them out by the spoken word of God in the name of Jesus! However they overcame their fears and overcame Israel, and consequently carried the Ark into a foreign unGodly place but look at what happens.

1 Sam 5:1-8 *Then the Philistines took the ark of God and brought it from Ebenezer to Ashdod. (2) When the Philistines took the ark of God, they brought it into the house of Dagon and set it by Dagon. (3) And when the people of Ashdod arose early in the morning, there was Dagon, fallen on its face to the earth before the ark of the Lord. So they took Dagon and set it in its place again. (4) And when they arose early the next morning, there was Dagon, fallen on its face to the ground before the ark of the Lord. The head of Dagon and both the palms of its hands were broken off on the threshold; only Dagon's torso was left of it.*

(5) Therefore neither the priests of Dagon nor any who come into Dagon's house tread on the threshold of Dagon in Ashdod to this day. (6) But the hand of the Lord was heavy on the people of Ashdod, and He ravaged them and struck them with tumours, both Ashdod and its territory. (7) And when the men of Ashdod saw how it was, they said, The ark of the God of Israel must not remain with us, for His hand is harsh toward us and Dagon our God. (8) Therefore they sent and gathered to themselves all the lords of the Philistines, and said, What shall we do with the ark of the God of Israel? And they answered, Let the ark of the God of Israel be carried away to Gath. So they carried the ark of the God of Israel away.

While Israel lamented the loss of the Ark, the word Ichabod (the glory of God had departed), spread through the camp and upon its unfortunate members, I believe this symbolises the church today without the presence of God or a Christian with out the anointing presence. Without His presence, there is no glory, it is Ichabod.

The Ark (Presence of God) was now in captivity but they were unable to hold it captive. It frustrated, destroyed and brought curses unto them, until they had no choice but to give in to its power. Likewise the presence of God in you will not cease to frustrate and agitate the presence of demonic forces in your life, and they too, if you continue to walk by faith, will eventually bow to the power and the presence of God in your life.

Eventually, the Ark ended up back in the hands of the children of Israel, in the house of Abinadab and King David organised a huge procession to bring the glory back into the camp.

2 Sam 6:4-8 *And they brought it out of the house of Abinadab, which was on the hill, accompanying the ark of God; and Ahio went before the ark. (5) Then David and all the house of Israel played music before the Lord on all kinds of instruments of fir wood, on harps, on stringed instruments, on tambourines, on sistrums, and on cymbals.*

(6) And when they came to Nachon's threshing floor, Uzzah put out his hand to the ark of God and took hold of it, for the oxen stumbled. (7) Then the anger of the Lord was aroused against Uzzah, and God struck him there for his error; and he died there by the ark of God. (8) And David became angry because

of the Lord's outbreak against Uzzah; and he called the name of the place Perez Uzzah to this day.

Just when it seemed that everything was going to be OK for the children of Israel we see a grave warning. David's men attempted to bring the Ark out of Abinadab's house but this poor fellow called Uzzah attempted to handle the Ark resulting in his death. When we consider this, we can learn something extremely significant about the anointing. God's presence in the Earth before the supreme sacrifice of Jesus Christ in the Earth would need to be handled exactly according to HIS stipulations, not ours, the consequences of an error would be as it was in this case, devastating. Without the atoning effect of the blood of Jesus Christ, we would have to endure the full effect of God's wrath upon our sin. Therefore Uzzah's mistake symbolises the judgement of God upon sin.

The children of Israel had been fully instructed as to the handling of the Ark and so, even as I write these words, I suspect that Uzzah thought that the rules pertaining to the Ark had somehow changed in the twenty years that it had been hidden in Abinadab's house during Saul's rule. He knew that the Ark had been apparently handled by the Philistines and carried away into a foreign land and therefore didn't hesitate to handle the Ark when he saw it falling, but Uzzah was wrong. God had not changed, the Ark was still holy and to be dreaded.

Today, people seem to have lost respect for the Anointing presence of God. Ministers squander it, behave disrespectfully towards it and even try to hire or buy it! Anointed ministers carrying the presence of God, have, in more recent times found themselves involved in scandalous public affairs due to the lack of respect for the anointing on their own lives. I suspect that as you read these words, many such people will be flooding to your mind. However, I write not to condemn them but to bring to a new level of import the presence of God in us through the Anointing.

If we are going to walk in it, we must honour and respect it. We must accept the perfect sacrifice of Christ which makes us as Levites (those qualified to handle the Ark or the presence of God). We must embrace the blessings afforded to us by His presence, by shouting a prophetic shout from deep within. Put this book down, right now. Stand up, go outside the house in your garden or wherever you may be and shout this great shout!

Shout "I am anointed with your presence" NOW!

The Bible records that Uzzah's perishing made King David most afraid. I suppose that was a reasonable fear under the circumstances. David's response was to send the Ark into the house of a man called Obededom the Gittite, who serves as a model of how to carry the anointing presence of God in our lives today.

2 Sa 6:9-12 David was afraid of the Lord that day; and he said, How can the ark of the Lord come to me? David would not move the ark of the Lord with him into the City of David; but David took it aside into the house of Obed-Edom the Gittite. The ark of the Lord remained in the house of Obed-Edom the Gittite three months. And the Lord blessed Obed-Edom and all his household.

Now it was told King David, saying, The Lord has blessed the house of Obed-Edom and all that belongs to him, because of the ark of God. So David went and brought up the ark of God from the house of Obed-Edom to the City of David with gladness.

Between these two scenarios, we see both the severity and the grace of God. Obededom received blessings and Uzzah, received judgement. Both are derived from the presence of the Ark, or the presence of God.

We have already looked at Gods judgement, now let's take a closer look at God's blessing. Today, the presence of God comes to us through the Christ Anointing, the presence of God through the Holy Spirit in our lives, and He brings with His presence, to the household of faith, the blessing of the Lord as in Obededom's day. So how do we define the household of faith? How does the Spirit of God manifest His blessing towards us? Let us look to scripture again. Let us turn firstly and principally to 1st Corinthians Chapter 3 and verse 16 which says:

Do you not know that you are the temple of God and that the Spirit of God dwells in you?

The Apostle Paul was addressing the believers at Corinth, he was wanting them to grasp a revelation of the dwelling place of the Holy Spirit, that in fact His dwelling place is not as we may have thought, the cosmos somewhere or in some religious sentiment but in fact His dwelling place is within the heart of the believer in Christ. Paul was saying both to the church of his day and also the church of today that you are the carrier of the Holy Spirit, that the very presence of God is within you and concordantly, the blessings of God equally belong to you. Please consider also the following scripture from the book of Psalms.

Psa 112:1-3 *Praise the Lord! Blessed is the man who fears the Lord,*

Who delights greatly in His commandments. His descendants will be mighty on earth; The generation of the upright will be blessed. Wealth and riches will be in his house, And his righteousness endures forever.

Let's analyse the description of the blessed man here, it will help us to define both how the presence comes and the result of the blessing. Firstly, the man fears the Lord. The word fear means more than just to be frightened of God, although it will behove some of us to do so! The word fear used here also means to revere or to have reverence for, meaning that you give honour regard and respect to the Lord.

Secondly, the blessed man delights greatly in the Lord's commandments. Let's think about that also for a moment. How can we delight greatly in the commandments of God in the Earth today? I submit that there is only one way to do so, and that is to delight greatly in his WORD. The Word of God, the Holy Bible is God's perfect will for man today. For the true believer in Christ, it is also our manual for life. Jesus is shown to us as the manifestation of the Word which became flesh and dwelt among us according to John 1.14. He also said that the scriptures declare of him, in the book of John.

John 5:39 *You search the Scriptures, for in them you think you have eternal life; and these are they which testify of Me.*

The man that delights greatly in Jesus Christ and the man that delights greatly in His word are one and the same. Jesus and His Word are one and the same also. So now you know for sure, if you love Jesus, you are blessed, and no matter what state your country, bank or personal finances may be in, you have a certain promise from the Lord. As long as you stay in faith for it, you can be sure of a delivery of God's wealth and riches to your home. You can take that to the bank for the Bible clearly states that they shall be in your house!

This was the very thing that occurred in Obededom's household. A careful study of the life of Obededom will show that he was a man who delighted greatly in the presence of God. Making himself constantly available for the Lord to use him in the service of the Ark. His reputation was such that David chose to send the Ark to his house rather that to bring it into his own presence. I believe David probably thought that of all the men he knew, this man was the most faithful. If he couldn't carry the presence of God no-one will be able to do so. Thank God, things worked out well for Obededom, he was blessed, and the blessing on his life serves as a model for the believer in Christ today. Even if you don't feel blessed, the fact is, you are! Even if your bank account says that you are poor, you can begin to say that you are rich! The anointing qualifies you for the blessing of God, therefore anyone who will receive the full revelation of the anointing by faith will receive the blessing that walks along with it, it's a matter of faith.

In recent times, I have noticed an increasing and unsettling dispute rising within the body of Christ. There are those who believe in, adhere to and trust in a message of financial prosperity and those who are bitterly set against it. So heated has this argument become that the church is now clearly divided in its opinions regarding this very hot potato. Those viewing from a secular perspective have created a negative description for the message which they now call "the prosperity gospel". Members of the church community have mistakenly adopted this name and are now using it to attack their brothers and sisters in Christ who believe in what they do not. Effectively, the argument is, to coin a phrase, washing the church's dirty linen in public view.

So what does this writer believe? Just back up a couple of sentences and see for yourself. I believe that the presence of God in any man who receives it by faith will produce blessings in his life. Including financial ones! Is this message sometimes overstated or wrongly preached? Yes! Do some unscrupulous so-called ministers preach with the motivation of getting money rather than getting souls? Perhaps also the answer maybe yes, however this does not mean that those who are walking in true and honest faith should lay aside their perfectly correct biblical views as a result of other people's misdemeanours.

In concluding this chapter about the presence of God, I would like to encourage you to think carefully before using the phraseology of the world to describe another's point of view. Rather than bandying about disrespectful terms like preachers of the prosperity Gospel, which clearly puts anyone who mentions the notion of biblical blessings through God's presence in the same category as a charlatan money grabber with no moral or biblical principles. Allow the Holy Spirit to bring a balance to your mind and heart. If you are preaching the gospel of Jesus Christ it will require funding. It will require finance. It will require money. You will have to fight battles against the powers of this world who will do their very best to stop you from getting those funds and that which you need to get the job done. The last thing you need is to be attacked by your fellow brothers and sisters. I have had the privilege of working alongside many anointed ministries both within the church and television arena. One thing that I can say with absolute surety is that when you are committed to the purpose of doing the will of God, preaching the gospel and setting the captives free and of course most importantly, creating dwelling places for the Spirit of God to dwell. Blessings and provision will come to you. There is no need to beg, manipulate or pressure anyone to give. When the true anointing of God is in town, people respond with excitement, love, honour and with their cheque-books. I would therefore like to close this chapter with a request and a new definition. Firstly then, allow me to make my request. Please do not be tricked by the secular world into using negative phraseology about Christian principles however apt they may appear to be.

Do not use the term "the prosperity Gospel", it is both unGodly and unbiblical to do so. There is only one gospel and it is the gospel of Jesus Christ. To suggest that someone is preaching another gospel is to both judge and condemn them which means that those who do so are placing themselves in the position of the judge, a position uniquely held by God the Father himself. I would seriously recommend avoiding that position. In praying regarding this matter in recent times the Holy Spirit gave me a new definition for such teachings. I now like to call it "financial well-being through the understanding of biblical principles". Now doesn't that sound better? Doesn't it make the argument far more palatable for someone from the secular or unbelieving community? The truth is that if we continue to speak negatively about God's provision for his children, we will, by default slowly erode the very blessing away. This is the reason why I believe many of us as believers do not see the wealth and riches in our houses as promised by the word of God. Perhaps it would be fitting to end this chapter with the words of the apostle Paul who said beloved, I pray above all that you would prosper and be in-health. If prosperity and health was good enough for Paul it's good enough for me and for any anointed child of God who is prepared to receive God's word by faith. Having said that lets move on.

12. The Word of the Anointing

Now we have reached another thrilling chapter together. Here we will begin to discuss the Word of the Anointing in more detail! By now you may have realised that we have visited a certain scripture from the book of Acts several times thus far. Well, we are going back there again now. I suggest you just permanently keep something lodged in that page so you can find it more quickly next time. The fact is there is so much revelation in this passage that we will need to keep revisiting it until we have extracted all the meat we can get! Now also remember that faith comes by hearing and hearing by the Word. Read the following scripture out loud if you can. This time we will complete the entire passage.

Acts 10:34-44 *Then Peter opened his mouth and said: In truth I perceive that God shows no partiality. But in every nation whoever fears Him and works righteousness is accepted by Him. The word which God sent to the children of Israel, preaching peace through Jesus Christ-He is Lord of all- that word you know, which was proclaimed throughout all Judea, and began from Galilee after the baptism which John preached: how God anointed Jesus of Nazareth with the Holy Spirit and with power, who went about doing good and healing all who were oppressed by the devil, for God was with Him. And we are witnesses of all things which He did both in the land of the Jews and in Jerusalem, whom they killed by hanging on a tree. Him God raised up on the third day, and showed Him openly,*

not to all the people, but to witnesses chosen before by God, even to us who ate and drank with Him after He arose from the dead.

And He commanded us to preach to the people, and to testify that it is He who was ordained by God to be Judge of the living and the dead.

To Him all the prophets witness that, through His name, whoever believes in Him will receive remission of sins. While Peter was still speaking these words, the Holy Spirit fell upon all those who heard the word. Then Peter opened his mouth, and said, Of a truth I perceive that God is no respecter of persons:

I want you to pay special attention to both the first and last verses in the sequence. In verse 34 we see the phrase "Peter opened his mouth" before he began to speak. I have often wondered why those words are there. My sense is that the phrase is pointing to the significance of the act, that opening his mouth will give rise to the spoken word, which the Lord wants us to pay special attention to. He proceeded to speak in verse 36 about:

The word which God sent unto the children of Israel, preaching peace by Jesus Christ: (he is Lord of all:) That word you know, which was proclaimed throughout all Judea, and began from Galilee after the baptism which John preached.

The final verse recorded above tells us that whilst Peter was speaking The Word, the Holy Ghost began to fall on all those who heard it.

In this we can see an undeniable truth. The anointing is transferred via the vessel of words! Not just any words but specifically speaking the Word of God. I remember when we first began to feel the call of Ministry over our lives. We were attending a Bible based church in Harrow, Middlesex, with a great Pastor, Rick Johnston, an excellent teacher of the Word. Whilst serving under that ministry, I felt the leading to start a home group, consisting mainly of friends and family. We started to study every Monday night at seven pm. Those Bible studies were really anointed, mainly because the main subject which we studied for months was the about the revelation of Christ! In fact, much of the content of this book was born in those early Bible studies.

I didn't realise it at the time, but God was more involved in those studies than I had ever imagined because shortly after that, he re-placed me back into the Christian television ministry, (Revelation TV) where I was able to share principles that we were studying in those Monday night meetings. We only had 3 or four on a Monday but thousands via TV within months.

The Faith Tree

God our Father began to teach me about faith during those days. My real faith journey began when we were studying the account of the fig tree which Jesus cursed. You could really feel the tangible presence of God in our front room that day. Whilst we studied, I literally pictured Jesus Christ speaking faith filled words like micro charged nuclear explosions!

I used to do a taxi run after the study to take friends and family home, and my sister in law Gene who we call Sis was the last drop off. Standing outside of her house, I noticed a beautiful tropical flower growing in her front garden which really caught my attention. I asked her what species it was, to which she replied that she didn't know but you have the same plant in your front garden. I couldn't remember seeing it so I turned to Seva my wife who said she could not remember seeing the plant either.

It was then that Sis made a comment that stirred my faith. She said yes you have got the same plant because she and my wife got them at the same time but yours doesn't bear flowers because it is a male not a female plant. Now to this day, I don't know whether there is such a thing as a male or female plant but something about the statement activated my faith. I remembered the fact that Jesus was hungry the night when he cursed the fig tree having found no fruit thereon.

I made an about turn to our house, and found the barren plant outside our front door just as Sis had said. It was just a mass of green leaves with no flowers. I am sure the neighbours thought we were quite strange anyway so the fact that we about to have a prayer meeting over a plant in our front garden shouldn't come as a great surprise to them.

I remember a moment came when faith arose in my heart, and then before I knew it, I was speaking the following words. "Plant, if you are a male then change sex because from this day forward, I command you to bear fruit, I want to see a beautiful bunch of flowers like my sister in law's so get on with it, start changing now, in Jesus the name of Jesus!"

The next morning, enthused by the chapter that we had been studying, I checked to see if the plant had obeyed me. I remembered that when Jesus cursed the fig tree, it withered immediately so being of high (and somewhat immature) faith, I expected instant results. My investigation was fruitless or so it seemed. Nothing had changed or so I thought anyway. I was about to command it again when suddenly the Lord put me under arrest! It seemed like he was saying you are about to commit a faith crime.

Have you ever had the Lord place you under arrest just before you were about to do or say something criminally stupid? The voice of the Lord came to me clearly at that moment saying "Didn't you do that last night?"

I knew exactly what he was saying to me through this question. He was telling me that if I did it in faith last night, doing it again isn't going to make any difference. If I was going to learn the principles of faith, I would have to start by obeying its laws. One of the laws of faith is that you have to believe it before you see it come to pass. I made a decision that morning that took my faith to another level. I simply said "I had spoken the thing and that was the end of it must now come to pass". That was simply that.

Beloved Friends, words are important. Especially when dealing with things of faith. I needed to change my confession towards that plant because I am no longer in the realm of believing for the thing to happen. I am now in the realm of expecting to see results based on the fact that what I have declared has already come to pass in the Spirit realm. After that, every day I went to check on the plant to see if it had obeyed me. For at least a month or so, it seemed like it hadn't heard my words. Many times when we speak faith filled words over a situation or thing, we may not see a manifestation immediately.

Think of it like planting apple seeds in soil. You plant the seeds in faith, hoping to see a resulting harvest. You have no idea whether it will happen or not but you believe that it will either based on what you have learned about gardening or the fact that you have done it before. You wouldn't panic if you woke up the next morning and there wasn't a fine young apple tree growing in your garden. Likewise we shouldn't panic if things don't appear to change immediately. You started in faith, stay in faith until you see the harvest!

I just continued speaking to that plant every time I looked at it. Now what I said was very important, I didn't keep on commanding it to change sex and bear fruit. Neither did I give it a telling off for not obeying my words. I simply kept saying "come on, where's my fruit"? I did this every time I passed the plant.

One day, in the middle of winter, Seva and I had just returned from a shopping trip, and as usual, I reached the front gate of the house and was about to ask the plant where my flowers were which had become my daily faith declaration over it. Suddenly I noticed something that looked different. I dropped my shopping and walked slowly over to the plant and there it was. There was a tiny bud right in the centre of the plant staring me in the face. I couldn't believe my eyes! This plant that had only ever produced green leaves suddenly had a flowering bud on it! Man alive!

We had a praise party over that little shrub, I shouted and praised God! You see, you need to understand. I wasn't looking at a shrub. Not at all, I was looking at my newly found faith. I was looking at a victory of the word of God over my every circumstance. I was looking at the answer to every future problem I would ever face. I was looking at God's creative power and a confirmation that I was his son. Jesus said, "if you abide in me and my words abide in you, you should ask what you will and it will be done unto you". Now, I knew that was true, Hallelujah!

Every day that shoot got bigger and bigger until a beautiful red flower appeared. I shouted and praised God daily.

BUT

There was something that I had not considered. It was something that would make a huge difference to my understanding of faith forever. This miracle happened in the middle of a cold frosty winter and this plant was bearing fruit! Of course, within weeks the flower was dead. I immediately understood my mistake. The Lord was teaching me a principle of the anointing. He was teaching me to speak anointed words in the correct context.

God was teaching me that I had spoken the word with faith but a little too much enthusiasm. He said If you are going to use my word, learn to speak it correctly! I realised my mistake, took some time to study on the internet about the timing of flowering of certain types of plant, and then, when I was sure I knew what I was doing, I revisited the plant and told it to bare fruit in the correct season, and of course, it did. Every year after that, we saw bunches and bunches of beautiful red flowers, born by my faith in the Word of GOD. Hallelujah! I had learned an important principle and my faith had been activated for the future. I realised that at last, the anointing in me was beginning to bear fruit in the Earth. My studies were NOT in vain.

The Faith-Plant! Outside our window

That was just the beginning, when I cast my mind back to the night my body was healed from that chronic tiredness, I realise that there was a point at which the transfer of healing power began to flow through me. It was the point when I opened my mouth and began to declare that I am healed.

Prior to that point I was fully convinced that God could do it but the question was: Would he do it for me? And furthermore what would I have to do in order to qualify for this great blessing? As I recall, there were three things that took place that night, all three revolving around the Word.

Firstly, I had a deep revelation of the anointing in me, which I would say was in a state of dormancy. Let me explain what I mean by that. It had been some 10 years since I had first received the revelation of the anointing, I studied the word, I believed what it said and that was that. Life kind of took over at that point, I got married went to work, lived life and just got on with things. The message was still alive in me, but it was on the back burner. After all, what did I really need the message of the anointing for? My burdens had been removed and my yokes destroyed, I was doing quite well and attributing my success to the anointing on my life.

Now I may not have been going about doing good and healing all who were oppressed of the devil, but as I said earlier, the Lord opened the door for me to be involved in a TV ministry, serving alongside my good friend Howard Conder. After some years doing this, we were able to launch Europe's first 100% internet delivered Christian TV channel called Faithglobe TV, so I was busy using the anointing on my life to preach the Gospel using every medium available to me. I saw this as the best way to use the anointing, so I put my heart into it.

From the very moment I received the anointing on my life, I was absolutely certain of one single fact: Christ in me was my hope of glory! The Lord lives in me! Please think very carefully about that statement because it can heal your body and set you free from all kinds of oppression.

I absolutely knew by revelation that the Lord lives in me and nobody on this planet could have convinced me otherwise. Even until this very day this is a settled fact in my heart. When you know a miraculous thing like that, it's only a matter of time before things begin to manifest as a result of it.

That was the first thing that happened that night; I remembered his presence in me when Seva gave me that word from Psalm 28:7. The second that the manifestation of the Word occurred, it caused an interaction to take place between the settled fact in my heart and the Word of God that I had heard through her. The anointing is a settled fact that will produce a blessing. Once believed and received, it will lay a foundation in the centre of your heart upon which you can literally build anything by faith.

Recently I was speaking at Living Waters Church in Beaumont, Texas with Pastor Benny Thomas, who happens to be one of my spiritual fathers. He wrote the foreword of this book. I spoke about the miracle by which I was healed on the first night of three meetings, the message was eagerly received. The next day I was praying for direction as to how I should continue the message when the Lord dropped a thought in my heart. He said "You could talk about Miracle Gro". (a plant food substance used by gardeners) so I did.

The next morning I began to speak about gardeners back in Britain using this substance to help grow super plants, drawing a comparison to the spiritual heart of the believer in Christ. To my complete surprise, after the service, another Pastor asked me whether I was aware that the Miracle Gro Company originated in Beaumont, Texas. A fact I was totally unaware of!

I immediately knew that God was helping me to understand another principle of his word which I am now ready to share partially with you. It would behove us to use the same analogy now in respect of the anointing. Just try to think of the anointing in you, as a bottle of Miracle Gro. It gives you the ability to grow fantastic miracles but just like its horticultural counterpart it needs something to work on. I am no gardener but I know that if you had a tub of soil and poured a gallon of miracle grow into it with no seeds, you would probably end up with nothing except possibly some weeds.

The Miracle Grow solution is designed to work with a living plant or seed embryo. Likewise, the Miracle Grower in your heart is designed to work with one single type of embryonic seed; the Word of God. The miracle grower could simply be called faith, which comes from hearing the Word, (Romans 10;17) but which word is it? I believe it's the same word that Peter spoke which we just read: How God anointed Jesus of Nazareth with the Holy Spirit and power... etc.

That was the word that caused the Holy Spirit to fall on all of those who heard it. It was the same word that Jesus spoke when he walked on the Earth, when he said the Spirit of the Lord is upon me because he has anointed me. It is the same word which you speak when you declare yourself to be a Christian, meaning one anointed like the Christ. Can you see it? The Holy Spirit in you is your Miracle Grower! Plant some word seed in your faith garden (your heart), feed it with the water of praise, worship and thanksgiving and just watch it grow.

How long will it take to grow? That is a matter of your faith. How great is your God? How easily can you believe? It could take ten seconds like mine did or a month, like the faith plant. It could take ten months or even years for others. It all depends on your level of faith. If the full revelation doesn't arrive with this book, you may need to take time to nurture your Miracle Gro garden, by studying the word of the anointing.

When the garden is fertile, it will produce a crop, likewise, when the anointing message has matured in you, it will likewise produce a crop.

You may now be asking "How will I know that the time has come to harvest a word?". Is there a sign that will let me know that my moment has come to release my miracle?

Amazingly, Jesus Christ answered these questions more that 2000 years ago. Hallelujah! For a moment let us consider the parable of all parables recorded both in Mark chapter 4 and Matthew chapter 13. The parable of the sower holds some ingenious warnings for us, which will help us to identify exactly when our crop is ready to harvest.

Mark 4:14 says *the sower sows the Word.*

Now, we know what the word is don't we? It is the message of the anointed one being anointed with the Holy Spirit and power by the anointer who is God the Father. Continuing then, we read:

And these are the ones by the wayside where the word is sown. When they hear, satan comes immediately and takes away the word that was sown in their hearts.

Watch out for the enemy! As soon as you begin to put your anointed Miracle Gro garden together, he will probably attempt to wreck it by stealing your seed. Even now as you read this book, your mind may be invaded with thoughts of doubt. You may suddenly find yourself fighting battles which suddenly rise out of nothing or perhaps it may be the feeling of being bombarded by a range of subtle distractions, all of these are devices of the evil one.

Mar 4:16 *These likewise are the ones sown on stony ground who, when they hear the word, immediately receive it with gladness;*

And they have no root in themselves, and so endure only for a time. Afterwards, when tribulation or persecution arises for the word's sake, immediately they stumble.

Friends, watch out for offences! Unless you get that word down deep in your heart, it remains only on the surface and can be easily removed. Notice that tribulation and persecutions begin to arise because of the Word. These may come through friends, relatives or loved ones. The fact is, the nearer they are to you, the more offended you may be. There is too much at stake here, don't let offences rob you of your anointed miracle gro garden.

Mar 4:18 *Now these are the ones sown among thorns; they are the ones who hear the word, And the cares of this world, the deceitfulness of riches, and the desires for other things entering in choke the word, and it becomes unfruitful.*

Notice this time, that the thorns or weeds were already present in the garden when the Word was being sown. Think of these then as things in your life that were already present at the point when you received salvation. The cares of this world and the deceitfulness of riches being the primary two. Like any other garden you will need to weed out regularly otherwise the Weeds and thorns will use up the nutrients in the soil (The anointing) which will mean that you have none left with which to procure your miracle! And, as the Lord pointed out, should the Word actually find enough nutrients to help it to grow, it will ultimately be strangled by the thorns. We must not let this happen in our lives. We cannot be surface level believers, we must be deep and our faith secured in the fact that we are anointed.

Mar 4:20 *But these are the ones sown on good ground, those who hear the word, accept it, and bear fruit: some thirtyfold, some sixty, and some a hundred.*

Finally, we reach the point where some seeds actually get into the good soil. In the book of Matthew, Jesus explains that this is he who hears the word and understands it. That man or woman, according to the Lord, will bring forth fruit in varying percentages. Interestingly, some are happy producing 30% or 60%, but if you are really after the fullness of God in your walk as a believer, you will want to see 100% return on all of your seed plantings Hallelujah!

Consider this, what is the fruit of an apple tree that grew from an apple seed? Answer: Apples. What is the fruit of an orange tree that grew from an orange seed: Answer: Oranges. Finally then: What is the fruit of a Word tree grown from a Word seed: The answer is "WORDS"!

Nothing happened until I released those anointed words by saying "I am healed". My miracle gro Garden soil received the seed of the word which grew into a Word tree that produced a healing fruit of the Word in my body. Glory to God! If I could write in tongues, I would write some here! Hallelujah! This was the third and final manifestation of the Word that took place that night. I spoke it and it manifested as true. Remember this phrase: I have a miracle gro garden inside of me, whatever I lack, I can grow.

Here is an equation that the Lord gave me to help me understand the process of harvesting his Word.

The Word = The Seed

The Heart = The Ground

The Tongue = The Tree

The Spoken Word = The Fruit

The Scriptural grounds for the equation are:

1. The seed is found in Mark 4:14 The sower sows the word.

2. The Ground is found in: Matthew 13:23 But he who received seed on the good ground is he who hears the word and understands it, who indeed bears fruit and produces: some a hundredfold, some sixty, some thirty.

3. The Tree is found in: Proverbs 15:4 A Wholesome tongue is a tree of Life

4. The Fruit: John 15:7 If you abide in Me, and My words abide in you, you will ask what you desire, and it shall be done for you. By this My Father is glorified, that you bear much fruit; so you will be My disciples.

Understanding this concept has meant a complete reversal of the way I thought about God the Father. For many of us, grasping this concept is not going to be easy, for several reasons firstly: We will have to unlearn some things that are entrenched in our understanding and have been so since the day we first learned to speak. In some ways it's going to be like pulling wisdom teeth. In other words, its going to be a very painful process.

Secondly, once the concept of God's indwelling Word is revealed to you, it becomes a target for the enemy as we saw in Mark 4:15, equally, if we are not grounded in biblical truth, tribulation and persecution will come our way, which, according to our Lord Jesus, is as a direct result of the reception of the Word of God. I therefore encourage you to take a bold step with me today, into the riches of the Glory of the Mystery of Christ. Come boldly with me through the doorway of revelation and truth as we proclaim the Spoken Word together. "I am anointed". Speaking the Word of God makes the transfer of the anointing from the inside of you, to where it can get onto your physical body or indeed onto someone else's life.

Speaking Anointed Words

Learning how to speak the anointed Word of God isn't achieved the same way as we learned to speak as children. In fact, we have to unlearn some things we learned in the world before we can move ahead and learn how to speak anointed words. The first thing we have to do is to learn the value of words. Words are very powerful. One day I was meditating on the subject of words and I remembered and old nursery rhyme about words.

Sticks and stones may break my bones but words will never harm me.

I rewrote this poem under the influence of the Holy Spirit, this is what he gave me.

Words CAN really hurt me

More than fabled sticks or stones

My words can influence great change

In LIVES not mine alone

With words my Father made all things

In Heaven, Earth and Space, therefore

Like God, I use my Words to change

My Life, My World by Faith

In the next chapter I am going to discuss the subject of being sons of God in detail but suffice to say for now "Sons of God inherit the character of their father. The original Hebrew text of Genesis 1.27 says:

And God made man in his own image…And man became Another speaking Spirit like God..

Amazingly, when we received the anointing, we likewise became speaking spirits made in the image of God. In fact, the scripture that really nails this thought was spoken by Christ and actually states that it cannot be broken. Consider this:

John 10:35 *If He called them Gods, to whom the word of God came (and the Scripture cannot be broken)*

Look at that, the ones to whom the Word of God came!! We know which word is being referred to here don't we? No, think again and if you still really don't, go back and read the book again from the beginning cause you missed it! Theological evidence suggests that the Lord Jesus was referring to the book of Psalms 82:6 which states:

I said, You are Gods, and all of you are children of the Most High but you shall die like men,

Hold on to your hats for a moment I am about to make a statement that may make you feel very strange. Before you can handle the Word of God, you must accept that you indeed have a God like nature. Religious folk will dismiss this book at this point just as Jesus said they would, and that is precisely the reason why mere religious folk sometimes don't get answers to their many prayers. This is the reason why Churches with a religious mindset are suffering dwindling memberships whilst the folk who are stepping out in the flow of God's miraculous anointed word are flourishing. The next chapter therefore will introduce us to the concept of being God's sons or Sonship. This is the way we learn to speak God's holy Word by first accepting Him as our Father.

13. The Spirit of Adoption

I am so excited to have reached this point in our journey through the word of God together discovering the truths about the Anointing. This is the point when things are going to get really cool. Yes I said cool! Being a child of God isn't all about fighting the devil. There are some really awesome benefits heading your way, even as you read this book. The most exciting part about the anointing is the divine purpose that it carries. We touched on the subject briefly earlier in this book but now we will consider in greater detail, the spiritual condition of Sonship. This is a legal term so once again, we will be speaking in legal language. It's interesting to me that as a young man, I had a desire to become a lawyer. I never saw that desire come to pass, as I gave up my legal studies in search of fame and fortune instead. God in his infinite wisdom made me a preacher instead and little did I know how similar the roles would be. We are dealing in the principles of eternal justice not earthly!

In John 1:11, the Bible records that Jesus came unto his own, and his own received him not, but to as many as received him, to them gave he power to become the SONS of GOD.

Ever since I first read these words, I have been fascinated by them because deep within the construction of this sentence lies several awesome truths about our Sonship from God the Father.

Okay, let's unpack this for a moment. Firstly, Jesus came to his own, to those of the Jewish faith but they didn't receive him because they already saw themselves as the sons of God. This was because they were the sons or seed of Abraham, and therefore the promised nations of the Lord that would come out of Abraham's loins through his son Isaac. However, this was clearly not the complete sonship that Jesus came to bring to the children of Israel, as we see through the writings of St. John who records an amazing heated debate between Jesus and certain Jews of his day. Let's pick it up in chapter 8 and verse 33.

They answered Him, We are Abraham's descendants, and have never been in bondage to anyone. How can You say, You will be made free?

John 8:34 *Jesus answered them, Most assuredly, I say to you, whoever commits sin is a slave of sin.*

And a slave does not abide in the house forever, but a son abides forever.

Therefore if the Son makes you free, you shall be free indeed.

I know that you are Abraham's descendants, but you seek to kill Me, because My word has no place in you.

I speak what I have seen with My Father, and you do what you have seen with your father.

They answered and said to Him, Abraham is our father.

Jesus said to them, If you were Abraham's children, you would do the works of Abraham.

But now you seek to kill Me, a Man who has told you the truth which I heard from God. Abraham did not do this.

You do the deeds of your father.

Then they said to Him, We were not born of fornication; we have one Father God.

Jesus said to them, If God were your Father, you would love Me, for I proceeded forth and came from God; nor have I come of Myself, but He sent Me.

Why do you not understand My speech? Because you are not able to listen to My word.

You are of your father the devil, and the desires of your father you want to do. He was a murderer from the beginning, and does not stand in the truth, because there is no truth in him. When he speaks a lie, he speaks from his own resources, for he is a liar and the father of it.

Let's establish another truth at this point. It is possible to be the seed of Abraham and yet NOT be a son of God? This is an important fact for us to comprehend. I believe that the Jewish nation today represent the natural sonship of Abraham, the friend of God. This is a fact whether they accept Yeshua Jesus as their Messiah or not. I believe that the Jewish nation today are still the first-born of the Lord, carrying the blessings of our Father in the Earth, which includes eternal promises concerning the land, inheritances etc. Having stated this emphatically, I must draw our attention to the book of John chapter 1:11 which states that the Lord came to his own, (the Jews) to offer them the ability and right to become the SONS OF GOD. This would not be a natural but supernatural sonship, not of this Earth but of Heaven! The Messiah was offering the Sons of Abraham their ultimate reward, the greatest promise which was the sonship of God.

Those born of Jewish extraction today are the sons of Abraham and as such, they are God's firstborn in the Earth. This is a very difficult thing to put into biblical perspective because it is difficult for us to understand the eternal mind of our God. A friend of mine called Simon Barrett, a fellow presenter at Revelation TV told me something that helped me to begin to put things in the proper perspective. He said that Christians come to God through Jesus but Jews must come to Yeshua though God! You see we must all come to Jesus (Yeshua), one way or the other!

The Jewish nation are appointed and blessed of God but the ultimate blessing comes through the Lord Jesus and his anointing. This is God's final solution!

In the above scripture, we can see the children of Israel of the time arguing that the blessing and sonship of Abraham was the way to eternal Sonship. We have one father, God they said. Through that statement, they were about to pass up on the supreme blessing of sonship from God through the coming of the Messiah or anointed one. They had waited for generations for him to appear and when he did, they didn't know him.

Now let me again clarify this statement yet further as I do not want to be classed as an anti-Semitic. I believe in the Blessing of Abraham, in its authenticity, power and origin from the father. I preach it, believe it and live by it HOWEVER I simply cannot ignore the words which Jesus spoke that we read earlier. "To them gave he power to become the sons of God". I would be proud to be called a son of Abraham if indeed it was my privilege and background however, as far as I am aware, I was not born of a Semitic line. I was born the son of West Indian Parents from the Island of Barbados. Their forefathers were taken from Africa as slaves, without any knowledge of the faith of their forefathers. In simple terms, in the times when Jesus lived and walked on the Earth, I would have been regarded by the Jews as a heathen or barbarian, which was the proper translation of the word "gentile".

so the word was sent outside of Israel for a purpose, to make those outside of Israel the sons of God.

I am in no doubt whatsoever that the book of Ephesians chapter 2 and verse 11 clearly places us as engrafted into the promises and the commonwealth of Israel. We didn't replace the Jews but we are engrafted into the precious promises made to them. We had to be engrafted in because God our father doesn't take back his promises or annul his side of the covenant. In order to receive the blessings of Anointed sonship, we had to be engrafted in to the promises made to Israel. That said, let us move on with the issue of sonship in Christ.

Christ makes us Sons of God

The presence of God in us, makes us to be called the sons of God. We serve a God of purpose. Everything God does, he does with a divine purpose interwoven within it.

Our next challenge, therefore, is to find the purpose for Anointing? Ready? Let's begin:

Now, we have already learned that the Anointer, the Anointed and The Anointing are made one in the word CHRIST. If we, therefore, by scripture, can find the purpose for CHRIST the Anointed one, then we can find the purpose for CHRIST the Anointing.

What I present now is my answer:

St. John, the Apostle said:

1 John 3:8 *He who sins is of the devil, for the devil has sinned from the beginning. For this purpose the Son of God was manifested, that He might destroy the works of the devil.*

He said the devil sinned from the beginning and the Son of God was manifested to destroy the devils works, In order to find the sinful works of the devil, we must therefore, go back to the beginning, in the book of all beginnings called Genesis.

If you have been a Christian for any length of time, you are no doubt familiar with the events which took place in the Garden of Eden, God made the heavens and the Earth and everything in it.

Genesis 1:26 *Then God said, Let Us make man in Our image, according to Our likeness; let them have dominion over the fish of the sea, over the birds of the air, and over the cattle, over all the earth and over every creeping thing that creeps on the earth.*

So God created man in His own image; in the image of God He created him; male and female He created them.

Then God blessed them, and God said to them, Be fruitful and multiply; fill the earth and subdue it; have dominion over the fish of the sea, over the birds of the air, and over every living thing that moves on the earth.

Just as God had spoken, Man had dominion. He was the King over all of the Earth. He was God's representative, the very presence of God, in the Earth. He was God's most prized creation. The first Adam was the son of God. Adam was to have total authority over every creature including the devil who was by this time, banished from heaven, and resident in the Earth in the form of the Serpent. The serpent saw Adam's great power and lusted after it and to this end, he cunningly contrived a plan in order to get it.

Gen 3:1-6 *Now the serpent was more cunning than any beast of the field which the LORD God had made. And he said to the woman, "Has God indeed said, 'You shall not eat of every tree of the garden'?" (2) And the woman said to the serpent, "We may eat the fruit of the trees of the garden; (3) but of the fruit of the tree which is in the midst of the garden, God has said, 'You shall not eat it, nor shall you touch it, lest you die.' (4) Then the serpent said to the woman, "You will not surely die. (5) For God knows that in the day you eat of it your eyes will be opened, and you will be like God, knowing good and evil." (6) So when the woman saw that the tree was good for food, that it was pleasant to the eyes, and a tree desirable to make one wise, she took of its fruit and ate. She also gave to her husband with her, and he ate.*

The Serpent had succeeded in his dastardly plan, by contriving and twisting the truth. He beguiled the sons of God, swindling them out of their birthright of kingship and dominion. This was part of the works that John referred to, when he said, the devil was a liar from the beginning.

As we read on, we see that God made an immediate declaration to the serpent regarding his works, this is so important for us to see because in this passage of scripture, the purpose for anointing is manifest.

Gen 3:14-15 *So the LORD God said to the serpent: "Because you have done this, You are cursed more than all cattle, And more than every beast of the field; On your belly you shall go, And you shall eat dust All the days of your life. (15) And I will put enmity Between you and the woman, And between your seed and her Seed; He shall bruise your head, And you shall bruise His heel."*

The serpent knew that God, being absolutely righteous, gave the complete dominion of the Earth over to Adam. God doesn't take back anything that he gives, because he would be unrighteous if he did so. Further to this, when God gives, he releases, so Adam had the right to do whatever he wished with that which he had been given authority over, even if it meant giving it all away. If therefore, he could get Adam to hand to him the authority, he could claim the legal right of ownership.

The works of the devil began here, he sought then and still seeks now to make the sons of God become ordinary sons of men, so that he can have dominion over them by taking away their right to rule.

Notice: God said that the seed of the woman would bruise the serpent's head, in this, God was saying to the serpent, the battle is not over yet. You think you have defeated MAN but I declare that a MAN will bring about your complete destruction.

The enemy, satan has lived in complete fear of that prophecy ever since that day. He twice orchestrated the genocide of firstborn Hebrew males, firstly, through Pharaoh, in the days of Moses, because the Jewish nation believed that their deliverer would be the foretold Messiah - Christ. Once again we see in Herod's time:

Mat 2:1 *Now after Jesus was born in Bethlehem of Judea in the days of Herod the king, behold, wise men from the East came to Jerusalem,*

Saying, "Where is He who has been born King of the Jews? For we have seen His star in the East and have come to worship Him."

He was told that the prophet Isaiah indicated the little town of Bethlehem, where Jesus was born as the expected birth place of the Messiah - CHRIST. In his desperate attempt to extinguish the CHRIST, satan, through Herod, succeeded only to confirm Messianic prophecy through this monstrous act.

The purpose for Anointing is to transform the sons of men back into sons of God, so that they can regain their God given authority over the devil and all of his works.

To evidence this statement, observe the following three scriptures:

John1:11 *He came unto his own, and his own received him not.*

12 *But as many as received him, to them gave he* **power to become the sons of God**, *even to them that believe on his name:*

Which were born, not of blood, nor of the will of the flesh, nor of the will of man, but of God.

I believe it is very important that we understand the issue of Biblical sonship. Let me explain why. We see from the scripture above that the Lord Jesus has given us power to become the Sons of God. The power referred to here is not the power that accompanies the anointing which we read about in our core scripture in the book of Acts. In order to define this power, we must refer to the original Greek translations as we did with the word Christ. Here, instead of the word "power" we find the word "existee", whose root word is exousia. It means legal right and authority. Examine the words of the scripture above carefully as they are often misread. It said that the Lord Jesus gave them power to become the Sons of God, meaning that he brought them the legal right to it. They would not automatically become sons of God, because the qualifier and first step towards being a son of God according to this scripture is to receive the Christ (The Anointed one). In conclusion therefore, legal right was important because without it, our adversary the devil would have somewhat to accuse God about. If you think about this in legal property terms, you can see it easily.

God owns the Earth but leases it for a time to his Son (Adam). The son is swindled and signs the lease of the Earth over to a confidence trickster, but as the lease is a legal document, and since the son gave agreement to it of his own free will, God MUST now allow the agreement to stand, however, he states emphatically that a seed would rise from the line of the woman who would have legal right to take the dominion back from the swindler.

Remember, since it was the man who was made first and originally given the authority and dominion, it was the man and his seed which lost the right to rule, but not the woman and her seed, who were virtually unaffected by the deed. To explain this further, imagine if, when Eve approached Adam with the forbidden fruit from the Garden, he rebuked her and put her out of the garden refusing to eat the fruit. The Bible would be a lot smaller today, I don't even know if we would have needed one! God the father would have (legally) and proudly provided another wonderful woman creature for his Son, after all, he still had more ribs to choose from! Joking aside, what I am implying here, is that when Eve ate of the fruit, she alone was affected by it. Knowing this, she enticed her husband to join her in her state of sin. It was only when Adam ate of it also that mankind became affected and bound by it.

I sense that someone may be having a theological nightmare right now so let us draw some conclusions based on Biblical fact beginning with what God did after the fall. All we need, according to the Bible are three witnesses to establish the truth so here they are: firstly, there is God's response to the situation in Genesis 3:17. Interestingly, God sentences the man and the woman separately. It is no more Adam and Eve, its Adam then Eve.

Gen 3:17 *Then to Adam He said, "Because you have heeded the voice of your wife, and have eaten from the tree of which I commanded you, saying, 'You shall not eat of it': "Cursed is the ground for your sake; In toil you shall eat of it All the days of your life.*

Notice, God makes sure to sentence Adam and Adam ONLY in his response. He said the Ground is CURSED because of you. Not Eve, YOU. Adam would have to eat of the ground in sorrow. (pain grief and toil). Also notice: He would not be cursed but only the Ground. Eve was not mentioned in the effect but only the cause. God pronounces a completely different sentence upon Eve when he says in Gen 3:16:

Gen 3:16 *To the woman He said: "I will greatly multiply your sorrow and your conception; In pain you shall bring forth children; Your desire shall be for your husband, And he shall rule over you."*

Since God didn't mention the ground being cursed in her case we can deduce that in relation to her deed, it couldn't effect the ground. Eve was significant but only to Adam and NOT to mankind. She enticed her husband to sin and that was what God judged her on. This is important because if God had pronounced a curse on Eve, a woman would not have been able to bear the Christ child Jesus. Hallelujah! Stop and think about that for a moment. He couldn't curse woman because he had a plan to use her through Mary, generations later. He also didn't curse man because a man would be born of the woman who will crush the head of the serpent. The Curse belonged to the Serpent alone as he inveigled Adam-kind of the right to rule.

At this point let me say that until you become born again, you are of Adam-kind and therefore you have no right to rule in life. Your Earth is cursed and you will have to toil in sorrow all of the days of your life.

Secondly, there is the first book of Corinthians chapter 15 which states:

1 Co 15:45 And so it is written, The first man Adam was made a living soul; the last Adam was made a quickening spirit.

Again, Eve's transgression is not mentioned so the same applies here, however the establishing witness would be found in the book of Romans, Chapter 5.

Rom 5:12 *Therefore, just as through one man sin entered the world, and death through sin, and thus death spread to all men, because all sinned*

Can you see it? By one man! It is by the Adamic man and him alone that sin and death made its entry into the world. Woman was spared from the judgement because she was to be used later to bring about the destruction of the devil's works.

Consider these words from the book of Galatians:

Gal 4:4-6 *But when the fullness of the time had come, God sent forth His Son, born of a woman, born under the law, (5) to redeem those who were under the law, that we might receive the adoption as sons. (6) And because you are sons, God has sent forth the Spirit of His Son into your hearts, crying out, "Abba, Father!"*

Understand this great thing. The Devil is still bound by the law of God. Whenever he gains some success against us, he does it by using legal loop holes. He is absolutely bound to obey it especially when spoken from the Word of God, the Holy Bible from the mouth of the believer. In this case, the case of the birth of the anointed one, (using legal terminology), Mary, the mother of Jesus was legal. Her womb was un-cursed, meaning that the last Adam or the CHRIST MAN was legally born in this world and that born again CHRIST MEN and WOMEN are legally the sons of God.

Power of Attorney

Now, are you ready for an awesome revelation? Some years ago my Dad became unwell, and certain family members felt that the nature of his illness was such that he would not be able to handle his finances himself at least not for a while. My brother who lived nearest to Dad, had to go down to the bank with a letter from Dad's lawyer and sign some forms giving him power of attorney over my father's bank account and estate.

Some years later, my Dad passed away and his remaining sons, (myself and my two brothers) were left with the task of clearing up his financial affairs, which we did as best we could. In the process, however, we realised something. The only one among us who was authorized to actually deal with the bank in my Dad's name was the brother who was given power of attorney whilst he was alive. Glory to God! The power stayed with my brother even after my Dad had passed away.

Likewise, you have been given power of attorney over all of your fathers' affairs in the Earth, because before the Lord went away, he left us in his will! He made us heirs to his estate and inheritors of his glory.

Heb 9:16-17 *For where there is a testament, there must also of necessity be the death of the testator.*

(17) *For a testament is in force after men are dead, since it has no power at all while the testator lives.*

Jesus left us his last will and testament called the new testament, he swore it in his own blood and then sent back a lawyer, in the form of the anointing (Holy Spirit) to ensure that the devil couldn't rob us of our legal inheritance. Glory to God! Hallelujah!

John 14:16 *And I will pray the Father, and he shall give you another Comforter, that he may abide with you for ever*

Again referring to the Greek texts we find that the word comforter is translated with seven distinct meanings, the most obvious and poignant being the term where we get the our word paralegal from. *Allos Parakletos, Paralclete, Paralegal.*

Can you see it? In matters of Law, you will always need a legal representative. Now since the devil is a legal loop-holer, the Lord knew that we were going to need a mighty counsellor who was fully experienced in handling the adversary's many onslaughts, so he sent one for us, in the form of the anointing, the Holy Spirit.

We have already covered the Legal side of things, in an earlier chapter. So now let's cover things from a more scientific perspective. We understand, In medical terms, that the blood type of the child will always follow the type of the father. Since Mary hadn't known a man, (Luke 1:34) she was to be overshadowed by the Holy Spirit, who would put God's Seed in her. In this act, God had been completely above the law, seeing as the Adamic man would have nothing to do with the new creation that was about to walk the Earth in the form of the Lord Jesus.

This new creature would bear the right and power to become a son of God. He would through his life, carry the right to also allow others to bear that right. He would by right, carry the Holy Spirit in the Earth. He would, by his death and subsequent resurrection, legalize mankind to also become sons of God with the ability to carry the anointing presence of the Holy Spirit. Glory to God!

If you are anointed, you are a Son of God. Claim it, walk in it, believe it and receive it. Do what Mary did right now, say yes to the Holy Spirit, allowing him to overshadow you, and birth in you, his son, the Lord Jesus Christ. He will not be born in a womb this time, but in your heart, the dwelling place of the Holy Spirit.

Amen

Mat 28:18-20 *And Jesus came and spoke to them, saying, "All authority has been given to Me in heaven and on earth. (19) Go therefore and make disciples of all the nations, baptising them in the name of the Father and of the Son and of the Holy Spirit, (20) teaching them to observe all things that I have commanded you; and lo, I am with you always, even to the end of the age." Amen.*

Through the anointing, you have the legal power to take down all the legal power of the enemy, it is as simple as that. Meditate on the above scriptures and allow them to dwell in you richly. It won't be long before that power will be manifesting itself in your life.

14. The Power Chapter

Luke 10:19 *Behold, I give you the authority to trample on serpents and scorpions, and over all the power of the enemy, and nothing shall by any means hurt you.*

I know, many of you have been waiting for us to reach this part, I hear you saying, OK OK I get it, the anointing IS the Holy Spirit. OK OK, It is available ONLY to the sons of God, but what about that POWER? When and how do I get it? How do I walk in it?

I hear you, so I am going to attempt to bring my perspective on the mighty power of God in the hands of the anointed believer. Interestingly, in my experience the power of God manifests itself only when certain conditions are met, according to God's word. In other words, you can't manufacture it by your own will, although it always operates in sync with God's perfect will for us. It is his power not ours! The power belongs to him. We get to use it because he wills for us to do so. I don't consider myself to be particularly authorized to talk about the power of God any more than the next man, as we all must believe and receive the power of God by faith. That is the only way to get it.

Secondly, there are two types of power, although in the English Language Bible, they are both translated as exactly the same word. The first one, we have already discussed in the last chapter, this was Exousia power, referring to the believers' legal right and authority. The above scripture from Luke is referring to our being given exousia. The other Power which we find in the Bible is called Dunamis power (miracle working power), ironically, in this scripture, this term is used in regard to the power of the enemy. I believe that is letting us know that the enemy does have some power to perform unusual acts in the Earth, however, we, as the anointed sons of God have POWER, legal right and AUTHORITY over all of his works, Glory be to God.

So the Exousia Power is the legal right and authority to wield the anointing and operate in the Dunamis (miracle working) power of God.

Going back to our core scripture, in the book of Acts, chapter 10 and verse 38, we see the statement:

Act 10:38 *how God anointed Jesus of Nazareth with the Holy Spirit and with power, who went about doing good and healing all who were oppressed by the devil, for God was with Him.*

For the record, the Power which accompanies the presence of the Holy Ghost, is Dunamis! Miracle Working Power! This is the power which operates in the life of the believer, by the faith of the believer.

Ephesians 3:16 gives us a deeper understanding of this power, explaining how and where it dwells. Ephesians three is without a doubt the official Anointing chapter, so we have included the entire chapter for your perusal here; Twenty one awesome verses about the anointing. Let's read it together and we will unpack it as we go.

Eph 3:1-5 *For this reason I, Paul, the prisoner of Christ Jesus for you Gentiles-* (2) *if indeed you have heard of the dispensation of the grace of God which was given to me for you,* (3) *how that by revelation He made known to me the mystery (as I have briefly written already,* (4) *by which, when you read, you may understand my knowledge in the mystery of Christ),* (5) *which in other ages was not made known to the sons of men, as it has now been revealed by the Spirit to His holy apostles and prophets:*

Well it looks like we are speaking the same language here doesn't it? The Apostle Paul, speaking about the mystery, really gets me excited, in fact it is in honouring of this verse of scripture that this book is named. If you have been reading along by the spirit of God, Christ is no longer a mystery but now it has been revealed by the Spirit of God.

Eph 3:5-8 *which in other ages was not made known to the sons of men, as it has now been revealed by the Spirit to His holy apostles and prophets:* (6) *that the Gentiles should be fellow heirs, of the same body, and partakers of His promise in Christ through the gospel,* (7) *of which I became a minister according to the gift of the grace of God given to me by the effective working of His power.* (8) *To me, who am less than the least of all the saints, this grace was given, that I should preach among the Gentiles the unsearchable riches of Christ,*

The riches of the anointing, the subject of this book, is now being made available to the Gentiles! Remember I mentioned this once before, that in the days when Jesus walked on the Earth, and indeed in some Jewish circles today, you and I (assuming that you were NOT born of the natural line of Abraham) would be called gentile or Heathen. Of course, now you are in Christ, that title has been utterly abolished, you are one with him, part of the new man in the anointed Christ.

Eph 3:9 and to make all see what is the fellowship of the mystery, which from the beginning of the ages has been hidden in God who created all things through Jesus Christ;

The word fellowship being used here is the Greek word koinonia which means partnership. The Apostle is saying you have a part to play in this mystery, it was hidden in days of old but now it is being revealed to you and I. The anointing doesn't work without three parties! You are the third person in the trinity of the Anointing.

Eph 3:10-11 to the intent that now the manifold wisdom of God might be made known by the church to the principalities and powers in the heavenly places, (11) according to the eternal purpose which He accomplished in Christ Jesus our Lord,

Notice, the writer puts the word Christ BEFORE the name Jesus on this occasion. This is to draw our attention to the anointing, making sure that we don't miss the point!

Eph 3:12-17 *in whom we have boldness and access with confidence through faith in Him. (13) Therefore I ask that you do not lose heart at my tribulations for you, which is your glory. (14) For this reason I bow my knees to the Father of our Lord Jesus Christ, (15) from whom the whole family in heaven and earth is named, (16) that He would grant you, according to the riches of His glory, to be strengthened with might through His Spirit in the inner man,*

Let's park here for a second, and soak in the glory! We already know what the riches are right? But look at the phrase *"to be strengthened with might by his Spirit in the inner man";*

The word might here is actually translated from one of the two power words we mentioned earlier, but which one? You guessed it! Its Miracle working Power, Dunamis! Remember a few chapters back, we talked about the Miracle Gro Garden? Well, there it is, situated exactly where we said it would be, in your heart of hearts in the inner man. Paul prays that we would be strengthened with MIGHT (DMWP! Dunamis Miracle Working Power) in the inner man so that the anointing (the presence of the Holy Spirit and power in the inner man) may dwell in our hearts by faith. Notice, the circle of faith, the anointing is producing Dunamis power, which, in turn is giving us strength to carry the anointing! In other words, that anointing comes with sufficient power to replenish itself from microsecond to microsecond.

Eph 3:17 *that Christ may dwell in your hearts through faith; that you, being rooted and grounded in love,*

may be able to comprehend with all the saints what is the width and length and depth and height- (19) *to know the love of Christ which passes knowledge; that you may be filled with all the fullness of God.*

Eph 3:20-21 *Now to Him who is able to do exceedingly abundantly above all that we ask or think, according to the power that works in us,* (21) *to Him be glory in the church by Christ Jesus to all generations, forever and ever. Amen.*

When all is said and done, the anointing works by Love. The scripture is telling us that when you fully experience the power of the anointing, you will be fully experiencing the Love of God. Let me expand on that for a moment. Thinking back to the times when God has really come through for me, providing miracles of finances, health, faith etc. I have always felt so blessed to know that God, the almighty took the time out to help me out. At that moment, I felt truly loved of God. That is the real power of the anointing, the fact that the Holy Spirit comes to help you. As the Lord himself said, he was anointed to bring good news to the captives and to set at liberty those that are bruised. Think about this. What is the good news to a captive man? The good news is that it's time for you to be set free! Hallelujah! When the son of God sets you free, you are not only free indeed, but you know of a surety that the love of God has come into your life because the anointing works by love. God is willing to anoint you because he loves and favours you. What an amazing thought. The source of the power of God which accompanies the anointing is the love of God. You want the power? Open your heart to receive the love of almighty God. I hope that you are enjoying receiving this word as much as I am enjoying scribing it. This is truly a life changing word of Dunamis power.

15. Effects of the Anointing

There are so many by products of the anointing, so many that we really don't have enough paper to hold the fullness of it. I have a general rule as regards things which I give instructions about which is that I never teach on subjects that I haven't personally experienced. My desire is to be a "real" man of God, therefore, my intention is to talk about some of the things which I have personally either encountered or have been revealed to me personally by the LORD.

The Kingdom of God

Jesus said the following words in the book of Matthew 6:31

Mat 6:31-33 "Therefore do not worry, saying, 'What shall we eat?' or 'What shall we drink?' or 'What shall we wear?' (32) For after all these things the Gentiles seek. For your heavenly Father knows that you need all these things. (33) But seek first the kingdom of God and His righteousness, and all these things shall be added to you.

Now, whether you realised it or not, if you have stayed with me throughout this book, you have been doing exactly the above, seeking the kingdom of God because the kingdom of God and the anointing of God are one and the same. Notice this awesome statement which Jesus made concerning the kingdom of God.

Mat 12:28 *But if I cast out demons by the Spirit of God, surely the kingdom of God has come upon you.*

Cast your mind back to our core scripture in ACTS 10, where we read that Jesus went about doing good and healing ALL that were OPRESSED of the devil. Notice, the presence of the complete Holy trinity is contained in the above statement. Jesus said "I am doing the casting out" but notice, he said he is doing it by the Spirit of God and that, Jesus said is evidence that the Kingdom of God has come unto you. He is still saying the same thing that he said in Luke chapter 8 which we read earlier, "The Spirit of the Lord is upon me, because he has anointed me. That has taken all of the mystery out of the term, Kingdom of God, because the Kingdom of God and the Anointing are one and the same. In simple terms, the Phrase Kingdom of God is merely explaining to us how things will operate by and through the anointing. I would really need to write another book in order to deal with this topic in its entirety.

Authority over the Enemy

Luke 10:19-20 *Behold, I give you the authority to trample on serpents and scorpions, and over all the power of the enemy, and nothing shall by any means hurt you. (20) Nevertheless do not rejoice in this, that the spirits are subject to you, but rather rejoice because your names are written in heaven."*

Jesus has given us authority over demonic powers and spirits through the anointing. His presence with us guarantees certain victory over all of the plans of the enemy. He warns us not to get over excited about the fact that Spirits are subject to us but he didn't say we are not to recognise and walk in our authority. Don't have a party about it, just know it and use it to the glory of God.

The Anointing on your mind

Right now I have some good news about the anointing. If you seek God for it, the Anointing can effect your mortal body in ways you may not have realised before. We already know that you can be healed through the anointing but greater than this, you could even receive supernatural abilities like Samson or Elijah. Remember what the Bible states in Romans

Rom 8:11 *But if the Spirit of Him who raised Jesus from the dead dwells in you, He who raised Christ from the dead will also give life to your mortal bodies through His Spirit who dwells in you.*

You got it? The anointing in you is the Spirit that quickens you! The word quicken is an old English word that means either to speed up or make alive.

One of the superheroes that I really admired as a child was the Flash. Do you remember him? He was an ordinary guy who somehow received an extraordinary ability to move at lightning speed, affecting the world around him in a split second. His world moved a lot faster than that of the rest of the planet. Likewise there was a movie called Clockstoppers in which a teenager finds an experimental watch made by his father, the wearer of which was afforded lightning speed whilst the world around moved with a very slow stop pause action. This was major Hollywood fun, and perhaps closer to reality than you might imagine.

1 Jn 1:5 *This is the message which we have heard from Him and declare to you, that God is light and in Him is no darkness at all.*

The Bible tells us that God is Light. Now, science tells us that light moves at a speed of 187,000 miles per second. To give you an idea of how fast that is, light could travel 2.5 times around the Earth before you would have an opportunity to blink your eyes! You may have heard the word Godspeed (an old English word) used as a kind of farewell. Since we know from the scripture that God is light, we now have a new definition for the term. Are you with me so far?

Now let's draw some further conclusions. Since the heavens are the realms of God, and since we don't see God, we can assume that everything in the heavens is operating at light speed and above. This is why, with our natural eyes, we are unable to see the heavens, unless quickened to do so by the Lord.

I believe that the Earth and everything in it, is operating below the speed of light, hence it operates at a much slower frequency than the Heavens.

The Anointing often quickens my mental capabilities so that I am able to understand the things of God.

Do you know that technically speaking, the fastest way to send computer data from point to point is to send it via a light speed network. Today, this is known as fibre optic technology. These are high speed information super networks which form the backbones of and run today's worldwide information superhighways, including the World Wide Web.

God has often dropped things in my spirit in a split second which took me literally months to unpack. It is as if God's infinite wisdom was being transferred to me in what seemed like a split second. Terabytes of information seemingly transferred via the Lord's infinite super highway of the info packed anointing. Just like in the Matrix movie, where Neo was connected to a world where he could achieve the seemingly impossible, believers are being jacked (plugged) in to the ultimate source which is God's wisdom flow which comes through confidence in his Holy Word.

Anointing on your eyes and ears

The anointing could be defined as supernatural strength which is, GOD PUTTING HIS SUPER ON

YOUR NATURAL! Meaning that with the anointing in operation in your life, your natural capabilities would be enhanced by his glorious power! Glory be to God! Another anointing reality or side effect for me is the eye and ear anointing. What's that? I hear you ask. Is there such a thing? Again, I would like to take you back to the early days of my spiritual walk with the Lord. I recall, in the final days of that meeting, where Dr Dollar was teaching on the subject of the anointing, when he started talking about the anointing that would come on your eyes and ears, if you received it today by faith. He had scripture for it too! He pointed us to The 92nd Book of Psalms verse 10, where we read the following verses.

Psa 92:10-11 *But my horn You have exalted like a wild ox; I have been anointed with fresh oil.* (11) **My eye** *also has seen my desire on my enemies;* **My ears** *hear my desire on the wicked Who rise up against me.*

Notice the words (my desire) have been added by a human translator, (indicated by bold here or italics in some bibles) which means you can safely remove them for clarity sake if it helps you to see more clearly. Remove both occurrences and what you are left with is:

My eye also has seen on my enemies; My ears hear on the wicked Who rise up against me.

As the teacher spoke, I was getting so excited because he was presenting the Bible in a way that made it come alive with thrilling consequences. The notion of knowing when evil was rising up against you was too intriguing to me. I thought to myself, anointing on my eyes? And ears? What must that be like? I must have that! I had no idea what I was asking for or what was to follow that day but when the preacher asked whether anyone wanted to have this anointing, my faith and expectation was so high that I immediately answered yes, without hesitation. He prayed five simple words, "give it to them Lord", and, well, I don't know how it affected the other people standing there but I know what happened to me.

Some time later I began to hear high pitched sounds at unusual times. I noticed that the tones would precede and event like meeting someone for the first time or before eating at restaurants, simple things like that. After a while, I realised that these were not just coincidental sounds but these heavenly and sometimes alarming tones were warnings. The person I was about to meet meant me harm not good. The food I was about to eat wasn't cooked well and therefore dangerous to eat and so on and so forth. Now, with some years having passed, the gift has grown to a level of maturity, whereby I recognise several different tones and their meanings. Everything is important. Distance, pitch, tone level and position in relation to the ear. Left or right is crucially important.

You may think this is strange, but those warning tones have saved me from destruction several times, in fact, that's how I know they are anointed! They are burden removing and yoke destroying warning tones from the Lord.

So I know what you are thinking right now, what is the scriptural reference for the tones? Couldn't the Devil be the one behind those tones and oh by the way isn't there a sickness that causes ringing in the ears? Yes, Yes and Yes again. There is a sickness associated with ringing ears. I have even on occasion suffered from it. This was something which I believe the Lord had me go through so that I would be able to tell the difference between the gift and the ailment! In point of fact, as I write this book, my left ear is being attacked from swimming ear! (we took a vacation to finish writing this book and I spend most of my time in the swimming pool on vacation), so of course there could be natural phenomenon causing ringing tones, however, the presence of God in me, will quickly identify the ringing as physical so that my mind can be at rest. Secondly, ringing ears have been mentioned three times in scripture, I always thought they were negative but in my experience, they are not. They are a call to pray, or to slow down, or to completely stop and consider your next move very carefully. Here they are First in Samuel:

1 Sa 3:11 *Then the LORD said to Samuel: "Behold, I will do something in Israel at which* **both ears of everyone who hears it will tingle.**

And in Kings…

2 Ki 21:12 *therefore thus says the LORD God of Israel: 'Behold, I am bringing such calamity upon Jerusalem and Judah, that whoever hears of it,* **both his ears will tingle..**

And finally Jeremiah…

Jer 19:3 *and say, 'Hear the word of the LORD, O kings of Judah and inhabitants of Jerusalem. Thus says the LORD of hosts, the God of Israel: "Behold, I will bring such a catastrophe on this place, that whoever hears of it,* **his ears will tingle.**

For me, the warning tones are real, and a part of the anointing on our natural senses, which can, if received by faith, completely transform the life of the believer.

In my search to understand this element of the anointing on my life, I found some references to the word ear in scripture to be most enlightening. The Hebrew Word "ozen", used at least 14 times in the book of proverbs, can refer to the organ of hearing or simply the word "ear". It also, however has a more substantial meaning which is "to have acute hearing by use of a focussed ear or even to have hearing like the ears of a dog". It sometimes can mean to literally hear revelation! It is used in several poignant scriptures including the following two.

Proverbs 20:12 *The hearing ear, and the seeing eye, the LORD has made them both.*

And, another one of my favourites:

Proverbs 4:20 *My son, give attention to my words; incline your ear unto my sayings.*

Further evidence of this type of gifting can be found in a study of the Urim and Thumnim, which were probably stones held in the Ephod *(today, no-body knows exactly what they were)*. One day we were having a bible study with a young man from the church who brought up the subject of the Urim with me. Well, I had never heard of such a thing and immediately rejected it. How wrong I was. I had to repent to him later on. You know sometimes we can miss out on the greater picture by having a closed mind. Anyway What do we know of the Urim and Thumnim? We know that the Ephod was worn by the high priests of Israel. We know that it afforded the enquirer a direct answer from God when they made request or enquired of him. Urim means light which is something you see, and Thumnim means truth, which is something you hear. For the enquirers in Saul or David's day, this meant that they could ask of God concerning a specific matter receiving a definitive yes or no concerning the matter! We can see evidence of this entire process actually taking place in the book of 1st Samuel Chapter 30

1 Sa 30:8 *So David inquired of the LORD, saying, "Shall I pursue this troop? Shall I overtake them?" And He answered him, "Pursue, for you shall surely overtake them and without fail recover all."*

Here we see a direct question being asked of the Lord, with a direct answer being given. Absolutely no sorcery is being used, this is a legal, Holy and scriptural transfer of information between God the father, the anointing giver and his servant the receiver. Even as I scribe the words of this book, the gifting is in complete full flow, directing my words with great precision so that they will reap a 100 fold harvest in your life.

How did the anointing affect my eyes? Well firstly let me say that having the anointing on your eyes may not mean that you don't need to wear glasses! Many times when I have taught others on this subject, the very first thing that they want me to do is to pray for their natural eyesight. Sometimes, if the Lord wills it, there can be a special manifestation through that prayer. However, in my case I am not sure that the anointing has affected my eyes in the natural at all. I have been however, blessed to see clearly into the spiritual realm many times. Remember, the anointing is God, via the Holy Spirit, putting His super on your natural. My natural eyes are now able to see things that I couldn't have without the anointing. As the Lord dictates, I can supernaturally see what I call Holy Ghost lightning's everywhere, forming shapes and directions. Sometimes they direct me, when to go or stop. The lights can tell me when to pick up my phone or wallet or when I should and when not to buy, or eat, or speak, or be silent etc.

The Lord uses the lights to let me know when people are happy, sad, arrogant, angry or untrustworthy. He uses the lights to correct my work, ticks for yes and minus for no. The vocabulary is huge and the rewards are tremendous.

Over the years I have shared this teaching many times, and people are blessed over and over again as their minds become open to hear the truth about this awesome gift which comes via the anointing.

There's a lot more that I could say, but if you are still sceptical, take a look at the account of Elisha's servant in the book of Kings. Elisha was a man of great faith but encountered with a doubting Thomas in the camp, he prayed a very special prayer.

2 Ki 6:17 And Elisha prayed, and said, "LORD, I pray, open his eyes that he may see." Then the LORD opened the eyes of the young man, and he saw. And behold, the mountain was full of horses and chariots of fire all around Elisha.

As I said earlier, the anointing will open your eyes to see into the realms of God. I have seen visions in prayer meetings, dreams and visions of the night. Open visions during church services, in my home and other places. I have seen many more manifestations of the eyes than I can speak of in this book. Pray and ask the Lord to give you this gift now, I agree with you, that it will be good for you, and that you will benefit from this effect of God's anointing that makes your senses super!

Put your hands on your eyes right now and say "Lord, please allow your anointing power to come upon my eyes though the presence of the Holy Spirit. I want to see what you want me to see. I receive it as done now, by faith, in the name of Jesus. Amen".

The Complete Anointing

One of my favourite scriptures concerning the anointing can be found in the 89th Psalm, take a look, we will unpack this one as we go.

Psa 89:20 *I have found David my servant; with my holy oil have I anointed him:*

Hallelujah! David was anointed by the Lord God almighty. Now before you start rejecting this message as Old Testament and therefore not applicable let me state the following. I do not believe that David's anointing is exactly the same as the anointing we walk in today *(if you are born again)* because in David's time, Jesus Christ had not yet gone to the cross. Salvation had not been fully purchased, sin not atoned for etc. This was the former and not the latter rain anointing. This anointing therefore was ON him, not in him as the Lord Jesus taught us. The good news about this scripture, however, is that we get a perfect picture of the effects of the anointing on David's life and therefore, the effect on ours also. We can learn so much about the anointing and the Holy Spirit because even though this was the former rain, it carries the same signature as the latter.

Psa 89:21 *With whom My hand shall be established; Also My arm shall strengthen him.*

The Hand of the Lord and the arm of the Lord speak of God's power and authority. It speaks also of his assistance. If you are anointed by the Lord, the Holy Spirit is with you to assist you with every trial you may face in life. This reminds me of the book of Acts chapter 11, in which we see a fledgling church being helped by the Lord. They were first called anointed or Christians in that town called Antioch because the Lord's hand was with them, Hallelujah!

Psa 89:22 *The enemy shall not outwit him, Nor the son of wickedness afflict him.*

By Far one of my favourite verses of scripture in the Bible!

The anointing protects you from the Devil!

By faith, if you are anointed, the Enemy is UNABLE to afflict you! That is a promise from heaven itself, to keep us safe from the wiles of our enemy. In addition to this, the son of wickedness is also restricted from touching us. This means that those who are under the influence of the enemy are also bound by the power of the anointing in our lives. I have seen this scripture actively working in my life many times when I have found myself close to being mistreated by evil people. Glory to God! We are safe in the anointing. Perhaps there is someone in your life and, when you think about them, a sense of fear seems to overwhelm you? Well, you can overwhelm your fear with the knowledge that you have the presence of the living God inside of you. That person doesn't have the authority to touch you or your life in Jesus name.

Psa 89:23 *I will beat down his foes before his face, And plague those who hate him.*

God promises to beat our enemies down for our sake! The Lord fights our battles for us through the anointing. Are you in a battle of any kind right now? Whatever your battle may be, the bible is showing us that if we know by faith that we are anointed, the battle is no longer ours, but God's. He is ready to face up to our foes, for our sake. Many times believers are tripped up by the lack of this knowledge. Rather than looking unto the Spirit of God in us, to heal our hurts and fight our battles for us, we choose to fight our own battles, carrying offences against individuals who have hurt us. STOP IT NOW! Release that person and allow God to fight your battle for you, after all, he has already promised us the victory in Jesus name. There is so much power in what you have just read, please don't ignore it.

Psa 89:24 *But My faithfulness and My mercy shall be with him, And in My name his horn shall be exalted.*

The word Faithful is literally translated as steady or secure, the anointing brings us the security of God in our lives. He is faithful and just to keep his promises through his word. God's amazing grace and mercy is ours through the anointing.

Psa 89:25 *Also I will set his hand over the sea, And his right hand over the rivers.*

Symbolically Seas and rivers are indicative of the people of the entire world, as the seas cover every part of the globe. This verse, therefore speaks of God the Father giving us influence throughout the World. You are anointed to influence the entire planet for Jesus Christ. This is another extremely important point about the anointing. The anointing of God makes you an influential person. As wonderful as that may seem, we must be careful to utilise our new nature appropriately. God has made you an influential person because he wants you to use your influence to spread the gospel of the anointing. The purpose is to bring others into the light and out of darkness. Misuse of our God given influence can result in grave circumstances.

Psa 89:26 *He shall cry to Me, 'You are my Father, My God, and the rock of my salvation.'*

This verse, of course speaks of sonship through the anointing, of course this is a subject that we have already covered extensively earlier in this book. The subject matter is revisited by Apostle Paul in the book of Romans when he talks about the Spirit within whereby we cry ABBA father. When I first heard the term ABBA, I thought what in the world is a Swedish rock group doing in the Bible? Of course, now I know that the word abba has nothing at all to do with music! It is a most beautiful Aramaic Hebrew term which is quite difficult to express in the English language. It is a term of reference so personal and private that it would only be used by a family member to another close relation like father, mother, grandpa, or grandma etc. In the simplest of terms it was like a pet name like darling or dada. This is another mystery of the anointing, it changes our relationship with God intimately.

Psa 89:27 *Also I will make him My firstborn, The highest of the kings of the earth.*

The Anointing makes me his firstborn? Higher than the kings of the Earth? It sounds almost too surreal but believe me, this is the truth. Now get ready, for I am about to say something extremely radical. Jesus said that we are Gods! And He further went on to clarify what makes us such! The ones to whom the word of God came and that the scripture cannot be broken. I know the English doesn't read that well but blame that on the translator not me! *(John 10.34)* Many may have problems with that line of scripture because you simply cannot identify with the life of a King or a Queen. However, I say to you now, begin to receive this word by faith, try to understand that we, in this life are limited only by the restrictions that this world has applied to us. In God's realm, all things are most certainly and absolutely possible. You are a King or Queen through the anointed one and his anointing from the Father God. Am I saying that we are God? No! A thousand times, NO! I am pointing out that Jesus said we would have God-like status in the Earth because of the anointing, Hallelujah! Praise God.

Psa 89:28 *My mercy I will keep for him forever, And My covenant shall stand firm with him.*

The word "Mercy" used here is the Hebrew word Hesed. This word cannot be translated with one English word. This is a covenant term, wrapping up in itself all the positive attributes of God: love, covenant faithfulness, mercy, grace, kindness, loyalty. In short, acts of devotion and lovingkindness that go beyond the requirements of duty.

God also speaks here of making us his firstborn though the anointing. This aligns perfectly with Ephesians chapter 2, where we learn that through the anointing and the shedding of the blood of the Anointed one, we are engrafted into the blessings and promises of Israel.

Psa 89:29 *His seed also I will make to endure forever, And his throne as the days of heaven.*

The third chapter of Galatians identifies the referred to seed for us.

Gal 3:16 *Now to Abraham and his Seed were the promises made. He does not say, "And to seeds," as of many, but as of one, "AND TO YOUR SEED," who is Christ.*

If you are anointed then you are Abraham's seed and heirs to the Kingdom of God and his blessings in the Earth, according to the promise.

As you and I grow in the things of God and in the knowledge of his Word, the anointing will become more and more of a reality in our lives. It will produce faith for the miraculous provision of God in every area of our need. The benefits that come from the presence of God are, in fact, limitless! Our challenge is seeing beyond the limitations of this world and grasping the revelation of Christ. We are further challenged with appropriating the blessings that Christ, (the presence of the anointing, which is the Holy Spirit,) affords us through his Covenant promises.

Selah!

16. Enemies of the Anointing

At this point, I would like to offer some words of caution. We have taken an awesome journey together haven't we? It has been a journey of discovery that has taken us deep into the Word of God. But, as with every long journey, there are always dangers to watch out for and things to be cautious about. Equally, there are some things that may cause us to lose the ability to walk in the fullness of the anointing, that is, if we are not careful. The enemy will set pitfalls for us to fall in from the second he knows that we are anointed with the Holy Spirit and power.

I may as well go ahead and deal with the obvious one first.

SIN

Of course SIN is an anointing blocker. But since the world is full of so much of it, we really have to be specific concerning this touchy subject. Now first of all let me make something abundantly clear.

I'm not going to be listing sins here in this book, or commenting on which sins I believe are worst than the other.

Christ came to deal with the works of the devil. The term the works of the devil is not just referring to any particular sin. it is referring to the SIN condition itself.

This, for a believer, is sometimes far more dangerous, even than the act of sin itself. The devil, our adversary has one major aim, and that is to rob every believer of his or her precious anointing.

The enemy will use every weapon in his arsenal of devices to achieve this quintessential aim. One key weapon which has proven to produce a result many times for him, is guilt.

You see, if the enemy can make you feel guilty about un-confessed sins which you may have committed or worse still, about the sin condition you were born in, he has won a major victory. He hasn't got to fight against the anointing on your life.

This is because the anointing cannot flow perfectly in the life of a believer who hasn't yet realised that his righteousness has been purchased by the blood of Christ. Man's sin condition has been completely and utterly paid for by the Lord at Calvary's cross. One who is truly anointed, has recognised this fact and is walking in the reality of being washed in the precious blood of Christ. My very good friend called Hector Cormack who lives in the Isle of Skye helped me to see that one day as we were sharing on the blood of Christ. He said "Once a believer has received the revelation of the blood, he can be completely free from sin because once the blood is in force in his or her life, the Lord regards his sin no more. Where sin prevailed, God now only sees the blood of Christ. God CAN'T see anything that he chooses not to. Concurrently since he has chosen not to see our sin, He cannot!" I know this is difficult to grasp but if you spend some time in meditation, you will see it clearly. Many times, a believer's faith and hope in Christ is crushed because they were unable to resist walking in a pet sin. Concordantly, such a believer may even concede to living a life way below their God given rights, because they do not feel worthy of walking in the anointing.

Let's get something completely straight, even if you were the best, most polite, most gifted and obedient believer in the world, with the initials JC and a Bible for every day of the week! You still would not be worthy of walking in the anointing. This is because no matter how good you may be, Jesus has a patent on the word righteousness, and as such it is only through HIS righteousness and the shedding of his precious blood, that we can truly walk in the anointing. You can't earn the anointing by your good works! I am not saying that good works are absolutely fruitless, not by any means, the bible has much assurance for the good works that we do, however we must get the anointing in perspective. I have met some wonderful Christians in my life, absolute saints of God but on inspection I found not an ounce of anointing power flowing in their life. The question is: Why?

Remember we said earlier that it was receiving him that gave us the right to become the sons of God. In other words, all we had to do is receive him and the legal right was freely given to us. There was absolutely no effort required on our part. The believer had only to receive him, and that was all that was required. Likewise, if you have been caught up in something that is robbing you of your confidence to approach God the Father and ask him for the anointing, be bold and receive this word right now.

Repent! Do it now, don't wait, get on your knees and pray to the Father in the name of Jesus. Tell him that you are sorry for your sin and receive his forgiveness deep down in your heart. Repentance is a major weapon against the enemy because not having the capacity to understand it, he is flummoxed by the power of the blood of Christ. You see, that blood replenishes itself from microsecond to microsecond. Never ever losing its power to cleanse and set the comer unto, absolutely free from the hold of the sin condition!

You have been washed in the blood of the righteous Christ of God, and it is the blood that makes you worthy. Now that you have repented of that sin, ask God the Father to help you stay clear of it, for the anointing sake. In other words, make an exchange with the Lord right now, ask yourself which is more important to me? The sin? Or the anointing? I assure you, once you have tasted this true heavenly gift, there will be no turning back to munching on the fruits of sin and death. I guarantee, you will want the anointing more than anything else in your life! Don't let SIN rob you of your right to walk in the anointing. Enough said on that subject, you know what the area is because the Lord has already revealed it to you even as you were reading these words. For more information about the blood of Christ I would always recommend an amazing piece of literature called the power of the Blood of Christ by Andrew Murray. If I have not been able to convince you of its power in this short passage, no doubt his writings certainly will. I hugely commend this work to you. Now you know exactly what to do before moving on to the next enemy.

Offence

Another major weapon that the enemy will use against us is the weapon of offences. This is by far, next to the sin condition, is the most used and best disguised of the anointing's worst enemies. During the Gulf war, I noticed that all of the US tanks were painted the same colour as the sand, since most of that war would be fought in sandy desert dunes, camouflage was the best defence for the tanks in action there. In simple terms, if you can blend your tank colour in to the background, it will be harder for the enemy to see you. Likewise, when approaching the enemy, it will be hard for them to see your attack.

Think about your walk with Christ as a battlefield. To our opponents, we are the enemy, and vice versa.

We must both adopt a strategy for victory. It would be extremely naive and foolish for us to believe that our enemy has no such strategy against us. The Apostle Paul said that we should not be ignorant of his (our enemy's) devices. One of which, is that he is an expert at camouflaging certain tactics so that we cannot see the true nature of the attack that is being mounted against us. Often times, the master tactic which he will engage will be to use people who are close to us in our lives to hurt our feelings or to offend us. This is because very often, we are unable to see that attack coming in advance, therefore we are taken by surprise. We guard ourselves against attacks from the enemy, but not from our friends or family members, after all, why would my they attack us?

An attack from a friend or family member forms the perfect basis for offence therefore the enemy loves to use this type of strategy. Its success rate is high because our defences are down and we are easily attacked from the inside. The enemy uses this tactic much like the fabled Trojan horse story in Greek mythology. Let us cast our minds back to a scripture that we looked at earlier in this book after the sower had sowed the word of God.

Mat 13:21 *yet he has no root in himself, but endures only for a while. For when tribulation or persecution arises because of the word, immediately he stumbles (or he is offended).*

Notice that the persecution and tribulation arose because of the word which was sown, and the believer who, although received the word with joy, receives it only on the surface level. The Lord here intimating that he didn't get his roots deep down into the Earth and therefore was unable to draw out the nutrients he needed to resist the attack. He becomes therefore an open target for the enemy.

Who is my enemy?

One major effect of the spirit of offence is that the offended person loses the ability to flow in the area of trust. Offended Christians no longer trust their Pastors or leaders the way that they should. Good relationships are based on trust, concordantly offended believers are unable to travel beyond a basic level of friendship or fellowship. The effect of this, is that everyone is kept at a safe distance, including those whom God has set in the offended persons life to be true ally against the enemy's advances.

Imagine what the second world war would have been like, if their had been no Allied forces? Perhaps we would still be fighting it today, simply because of mistrust. Today's financial markets are in a quandary for the exact same reason. A loss of trust between each other is creating a lose lose scenario for everyone. Apart from the ever present nuclear threat, chemical warfare is perhaps the most frightening of all methods of war. The thought that you and I could be innocently going about our business in life, unknowingly breathing in deadly poisons designed in a laboratory with the ultimate purpose of destroying you and your family whilst wickedly leaving the buildings intact. It is without a shadow of doubt, a most sinister evil. In this comparison, we see the true menace of the attack from the Spirit of offence.

The enemy laps it up, he loves to feed us his devious concoctions of lies and deceit, camouflaged in our feelings of hurt and pain. He surreptitiously releases vile toxins of evil, which if untreated will ultimately rob us of the anointing on our lives.

I'm not offended!

The enemy uses people to: ATTACK US, SPEAK ILL OF US, STEAL FROM US, ROB US AND HURT US. He will use any and everybody through whom he can bring an evil attack against us in the hope that we will become so enraged or offended by the situation that we will choose not to forgive our assailants. Then he has most certainly won the battle because un-forgiveness is most definitely, an anointing robber.

I have personally watched this subtle attack at work many times. This is the one which undoubtedly destroys more Christian relationships than any other, because the nature of the offence can be so subtle.

As a Pastor, I have seen a number of people walk away from Church because they were offended at the Pastor or one of the other ministers. Some became offended with me. Usually, this was because they were unable to take correction from me, so they chose the offence route.

The amazing thing about each case is that they will always have a word from God (never man) that upholds their erroneous position. The enemy knows that this absolutely discounts me from counselling them any further because a word from God is clearly above my authority. I will never challenge anyone who claims that God has spoken to them, as it is their right to hear directly from him. All you can do is point them towards the right scripture to see if they might take heed, however, once the spirit of offence has taken root, it is very difficult to shift. The offended party therefore, leaves one church only to carry the offence elsewhere. When they arrive at a new destination, like a dangerous flu virus they will unwittingly seek to pollute another church with exactly the same poison. This is indeed one of the most subtle anointing blockers because it has a dual effect. Part of the poison will be carried by the offended but they will often seek to leave some poison with the offender. In other words, they will often leave you wondering what you have done? And why they have suddenly cut you off from communication? The offender, (often completely innocent) may spend days, weeks or months agonising over the split, trying to make amends wherever he or she can, of course this will be to no avail, as part of the enemies' strategy will be to ultimately offend you also, though this act. Believe me when I say this is a demoniacally assembled cocktail of occurrences which organically grows like a spiders web, ensnaring as many as possible to ultimately block up and stop the flow of anointing in their lives.

Delivered from Offence

I remember some years ago I had been involved in a business deal, which went sour and caused a deep split between myself and another Christian brother. We had been quite close over the years but this fall out was to cause major stumbling blocks in my life at the time. The brother made some very poisonous comments about my character, which I felt, were completely unfounded. Much of the problems which we were facing were nothing at all to do with me or my conduct but as a direct result of the enemy's interjection. I was very angry by his reactions, largely because he was apparently blind to the enemy's obvious attacks. Consequently, I sat religiously rehearsing my pain every night. By this I mean, I went over and over events in my mind, ceaselessly running through the bad things that had happened, and the hurtful things which he had said about me. I kept asking myself how could my former business partner be behaving this way towards me?

One day, I was alone in my flat trying to pray concerning the situation, when, once again, the anger and bitterness rose up in me to the point where I literally started to feel ill. Realising that I was being weakened by the thought of it, I tried to lie down on my carpet floor and just rest my mind. Before I knew what was happening, I had fallen into a deep trance like vision. My eyes were shut fast, but seemingly open, in other words, I could see the room with my eyes closed. I saw what appeared to be a spider (large Black Widow looking) appear lodged on my right arm. I have to say this vision more that concerned me, not being particularly fond of spiders at all. I yelled and tried hopelessly to get the spider off but it wasn't shifting. By this time, the talons had sunk deep into the flesh of my right arm. It was ripping at my very flesh and bones! I was petrified by this vision which seemed so real. I started to seriously panic wondering what this spider would do to me. The Lord had opened my eyes so that I could actually see the thing that was making me ill. I saw the result of my rehearsals and it was the ugliest and most frightening thing that I have ever seen.

I cried out to God in fear! I shouted, help me Lord! Take this spider off me please, please!! The pride had gone, the hurt had gone, all I wanted now was this thing off of my arm. The voice of the Lord answered me immediately saying, "You have caused this to come upon yourself". How? I answered. What is causing it to come? Please help me. I cried out again as the talons seemed to grip tighter into my arm. Once again, the voice answered with a single sentence, "This is offence! Unless you cut it loose from your life, you cannot walk in the anointing, in fact, you may even miss my call on your life and even the afterlife".

Now the Lord had my 100% attention. These words brought an instant chill throughout my spirit. I had read a book by John Bevere called the Bait of satan on the subject of offence, so I knew exactly what it was, but it had sneaked up on me, and tricked its way into my life. To think, I knew what offences could do to the anointing on my life but I couldn't stop myself from being offended. I felt completely helpless against this strong spirit of offence and now I was looking directly at it, in the spiritual form of one of the ugliest things in the world to me, that huge black widow like spider. I began to weep and repent of carrying offences against the brother. I offered every painful thought in my heart to God that day. I literally grabbed them out of me and handed them to the Lord, and he took them all away. I looked down at my arm and although the spider was still there, it didn't look as menacing, its grip seemed to be loosening. Then in an almost Hollywood like sequence, I looked down and saw a beautifully decorated golden small sword appear right in front of me, (man, when I think of this, I think God would make an awesome film Director!)

It was one of the most beautiful sights that my eyes had ever beheld. It had a white ivory handle decorated with gold and rare stones with a sparkling shiny golden blade. I heard an audible voice saying "Son, pick up the weapon and cut the spider loose". I picked up the small sword and proceeded to snap the talons off of my arm one by one, clink, clink, was the sickening sound that I heard. I was disgusted at myself having allowed this demonic thing into my life. Using the serrated edge of the sword I carved more expediently as each of the talons had to be rigorously worked for a moment before it would finally snap. Eventually when the last talon was cut, the spider fell to the ground, and at that point, I knew I had released the brother from all offences, I prayed for him and asked God to forgive me for carrying offence. I felt the sweet presence of the Lord sweep into my room that day. He literally took that offence right out of my heart and nailed it to the cross of Calvary, Hallelujah!

Ever since that day, I have been a recruit in the army against satanic offence. I love the words spoken by Apostle Paul nearing the end of his ministry, that he lived his life without offence towards man or God.

From the amplified bible it reads:

Act 24:16 *Therefore I always exercise and discipline myself [mortifying my body, deadening my carnal affections, bodily appetites, and worldly desires, endeavouring in all respects] to have a clear (unshaken, blameless) conscience, void of offence toward God and toward men.*

Now, let's get down to the root of it. Did I have reason to be angry and bitter with the brother? Oh yes I did! Did he do me wrong? Absolutely! BUT, it was all a design of God, to teach me how to handle offences. There was a divine purpose in that experience, it was bringing me wisdom that I could pass on to many others in life. Now I can thank God for allowing my friend to hurt me and to have been used in my life in this way. I take peace from the experience by knowing that satan lost that battle, by and through the power of the anointing on my life.

If you have truly received the contents of this book thus far, and truly want to walk in the anointing. Search your heart right now, see whether they may be an area of offence that you have held on to, and decide that you are not going to let that thing rob you of the anointing.

Pray to God the Father, ask him to remove it from your life and to forgive you for the sin of holding offence against another. People have all kinds of excuses for holding on to offence, they say things like, time will heal it, and it will work itself out one day or something like that. They walk around with it on a leash feeding it three bowls of milk every day. Listen, offence isn't a pet so don't pet it! Get rid of it! Learn from my mistake, do it now, don't wait to see that spider as I did. It was the mercy of the Lord that I should have seen it but I never would have, without the anointing on my life, upon my eyes and ears. Without this, perhaps today I would be lost. Selah!

Another primary weapon that the enemy uses against us is the spirit of pride.

The Spirit of Pride

Pride is most definitely an anointing blocker according to Ezekiel 28:15 lucifer was created perfect in all his ways, but iniquity was found in him.

You know it was pride that puffed lucifer up and caused him to lose a type of the anointing which he had. The bible called him the anointed cherub, a leader of worship in the heavenlies, but somewhere along the way, he started regarding himself a little too highly. Saints of God, we must be careful, as the anointing grows stronger on our lives, that we do not give rise to the spirit of pride. Keep things in perspective. Remember, pride comes before a fall. Walk in the awareness that Christ Jesus is our righteousness, and that we are nothing with out him. Our righteousness is like filthy rags before him as the prophet Isaiah said. Pride of life is what caused lucifer's fall, so watch out for that also. Be happy and honoured about the fact that you're a son of God but keep the pride in perspective.

Remember that even the blameless Christ was stripped of all pride when he went to the cross for our sakes and that you are only made worthy by the blood of his great sacrifice.

I believe pride is dangerous because it is generated by a spiritual force. Notice I called it a Spirit of Pride. Many times, I have noticed that people suffering an attack from this particular Spirit have no idea that they are being oppressed by it. They seem to display a level of self blindness which absolutely will NOT budge until it is openly challenged.

The Spirit of pride can lurk in a believers' life for years, surreptitiously camouflaging itself in the colours of a person's psyche. It is an ugly spirit that our father will not put up with. In fact, I believe the moment he gets a whiff of it, he sends us instantly to the spiritual shower to get cleansed in the blood of Jesus. He will do anything, absolutely anything to get that spirit clear of his children. This is one of the reasons, the Jews spent generations teaching their children about the pre passover search for Chametz. This was part of the Holiest celebration of the year in the Jewish calendar. The Children of Jewish households would be part of a rigorous search for every piece of yeast in a home. For seven days the house would be completely inspected and cleansed. At the end of the search the local rabbi would declare that the house is free of Chametz and take away the bread and yeast products. These would be given away or sold to another people not of Jewish extraction. (often sold back after the Passover). I hear you asking WHY??? When the Lord Jesus walked the earth, he understood only too well about the traditions of the Jews. He told them to beware of the "Pride", yeast, leaven or Chametz of the Pharisees! Do you see it? He was talking about pride in their lives. As the nation of the chosen, they had reason to be boastful against their fellow man, but the Lord warned them against it. Likewise, as your brother in the Anointed and his anointing, I would do the same. I would warn you to be careful of the spirit of Pride. You are anointed but don't let it go to your head! Keep it in your heart where it belongs. Every time you take Lord's supper, remember that He gave that tradition to us during or after the Jewish seder of passover, therefore, it has great relevance to us also.

When we break and eat the body of Christ, we should also search our heats for pride in our lives. We should beware of pride at all times as believers in Christ.

Reviewers Note: See Book of Job 41:34 The Spirit of Pride has a name: Leviathan!

17. Proper Motivation

My final thought to you concerning the anointing is this. What is your motivation for receiving the anointing on your life? Ask yourself now: Why do you want it? The truth is, we all have to be very careful about our motivation because it is easy to get confused in this area. We start out with the best intentions but somehow the good intentions of our heart can become distorted by the patterns of this world. There is absolutely NOTHING more wonderful than the feeling of being in a church meeting or a Hospital bedside, and having the anointing power of God suddenly coursing through you, as you pray for someone who is sick or bound by the Devil. Instantly, you know that this one has received his or her healing at your hands. I've seen many men and women who have been mightily used of God, lose balance through this feeling. I have seen them begin to speak about the anointing as if it were their own. Confidently, they begin to boast about the anointing on their own lives, taking the glory away from our Father who, after all, is the giver of the anointing. I believe these errors are caused primarily by a misunderstanding brought about by incomplete teaching on the subject.

In recent years, we have seen many prominent ministries falling from a place of grace and respect throughout the Body of Christ. A ministry fall becomes big news to the secular world which means that they are being disgraced openly for all to see. This writer believes that this spirit which we shall simply call "the spirit of me, myself and MY anointing", is another key contributor to the root cause of the fall. Unfortunately, it seems to me that some ministers have become so close to this spirit, that they literally welcome the self satisfaction and pleasure that they receive in return from it. It attaches itself to their psyche and becomes entrenched in their own thinking. This is a serious problem because now the Lord himself is unable to get through with corrective measures. The pathway for this man or woman of God will lead directly to a fall. I present this as one of the primary reasons for ministry failure today.

I pray that this book will, above all else, give clear direction as to where the anointing comes from. To whom the anointing belongs and how and why it manifests itself in our lives.

Clearly by now, you and I know that the anointing is more than just "POWER". More than just a presence or goose bumps, but that the anointing is the presence of God himself in our lives and as such it cannot be manipulated, abused or misused. Let us, together, pray to God our Father that we may walk worthy of the anointing presence in our lives. That he may give unto us, the riches of the glory of the mystery that is now being made manifest through the awesome works of his son, our Lord Jesus Christ. That we may walk in his precious anointing both here in the Earth and as long as we all shall live.

18. The Challenge

God's ways are so unlike ours, therefore when we begin to understand the mystery of the anointing, a challenge often ensues. The more that he reveals to us, the more it becomes our responsibility to walk in the revelation of it. As the many layers of the anointing truth were made available to me, the more I had to adapt and grow as a believer. God always reveals his anointing with a divine purpose! Just like a seed of faith, the anointing grows as we live with our God.

The Purpose of the anointing is to produce Christ like character in us. Whether that be in our walk of faith or our love walk and patience etc. As the anointing is unveiled, it will bring certain Christ like challenges to our walk. Don't despise them for they are necessary for our perfecting in the anointing. We, like Christ, will have to pick up our cross and follow him.

I once heard a well known preacher say "The Anointing will either make you or break you". My truth is a little of both, in other words, the anointing on my life is both making me and breaking me! Think about wild horses for a moment, I am no expert but I know that before a horse can be ridden by a Jockey, it must be broken. Broken means that the animal must be taught that its will is no longer the law and that it must obey the will of another. This is because before the horse had been captured, it was completely wild. It had a completely free will to do whatever it liked, whenever it wanted to. It had no master and made its own law.

Doesn't that sound like you and I before we became believers? Likewise, before the anointing was revealed to us, our flesh had a free run over our will. The flesh did anything it willed to do, whenever it wanted to. There was no God, no Lord and no Christ in us, therefore, we became our own law unto ourselves.

According to Ephesians chapter 2, we were without God and hope in the world. But after Christ, the anointing came, we have a knowledge of God, of his Lordship, his grace and his favour. We discover that we are his sons and that He is our real heavenly Father. We find out that our lives are no longer our own and that it is no longer US that live but Christ who is living through us.

The Apostle Paul draws our attention to something important whilst writing to the believers in the fifth chapter of Galatians. Not wanting them to return to the bondage of walking under the Law. He encourages them rather to walk in the Spirit, because by doing so, they will not manifest the works of the flesh. Likewise, we are challenged by the Spirit of Christ in us to walk after the Spirit of God and not to fulfil the lusts of the flesh. The challenge of the anointing is this: The flesh is powerfully deceptive and if we are not careful, we can be deceived by it, finding ourselves once again walking under its influence, even as believers.

Gal 5:19-21 *Now the works of the flesh are evident, which are: adultery, fornication, uncleanness, lewdness, (20) idolatry, sorcery, hatred, contentions, jealousies, outbursts of wrath, selfish ambitions, dissensions, heresies, (21) envy, murders, drunkenness, revelries, and the like; of which I tell you beforehand, just as I also told you in time past, that those who practice such things will not inherit the kingdom of God.*

Remember, we have an enemy, who is fully aware of our decision to walk with Christ. Just as it is God's will for us to walk in his anointing, it is satan's will to lead us away from doing so. He will set traps and assignments against us in various forms with the sole intention of getting us off track. Every word you declare will be challenged. Every prayer fought against. Every decision for Christ, impaled by tests and temptation. All for the satanic purpose of robbing you of your God given anointing. Watch especially for attacks of offences as I mentioned a few words back, for these are great anointing robbers. Many a believer has lost the wondrous provision of God in this world and even the next by missing this subtle trick of the enemy.

Watch out for those who are nearest to you for it is often through these, both saved and unsaved, that offences will come into your life. Anointed marriages will come under great attack, consequently, anointed believers MUST fight the fight of faith in their homes and their marriages. You will be tempted and tried in your personal lives. Every aspect of your character which has not been proven, will be put to the test. Your temperament and love will be pushed to the max and many times you will feel like giving up the walk but I want to encourage you with these words.

The Anointing is worth it! The Anointing is worth it! The Anointing is worth it! The Anointing is worth it! The Anointing is worth it! The Anointing is worth it! The Anointing is worth it! The Anointing is worth it! The Anointing is worth it! The Anointing is worth it! The Anointing is worth it!

The Anointing is worth it!

I would rather have God's precious anointing on my life than to draw back into the world and the things thereof. I would rather forgive than to hold malice and lose the anointing. It is the anointing that is on the line here, not just your ego. God is truth and the devil is a LIAR! He will send evil spirits to whisper lies about your faith, your family, your spouse, your children. He will plot against you and bring evil tidings against your name. He will scandalise and try to shame you,. Why? Because you are anointed! He doesn't want you walking in power and authority over him and his demonic works BUT you have the VICTORY! You have a recompense and a great reward! You can love those who hurt and abuse you. You can forgive those who do you harm. You CAN go on because you know the anointing is worth it.

The Power of anointing flows from your confidence in God. In other words, the more confident you are in his presence with you, the more the anointing power can flow in our lives.

The enemy aims to bring us into condemnation so that our confidence towards God will be marred. His desire is to break the channels of communication between us and our God by utilising the oldest trick in the book: Sin. He will use it to trip us up and then use the guilt of it to break our relationship with the Father. He has been using this method against believers in Christ, since the beginning of Christianity so he knows exactly what he is doing.

You also, therefore, will need to know and understand what you are doing. You will need to walk in constant relationship with the Anointing. You will need to keep the Word of God in your hearts at all times, walking always in the knowledge of his salvation and his amazing grace towards us. Above all, have confidence in his Blood, and its power to cleanse us from sin and the guilt thereof. So that should the day of failure come, (and it probably will). You and your anointing may be restored.

I write these final words unto you because I understand that the revelation of the anointing is an exciting one and that as the parable of the sower reveals unto us, some of us have a tendency to get excited about it without having the deep roots of Godly life experience to balance the joy with reality. Having faced many days of trials and tests, and of joy and Victory, I believe that I am at least in part, qualified to leave these sobering words with you.

19. The Beautiful Spirit

Beloved Friends, we seem to have reached the final chapter of this book, and we are ready to begin our anointed walk with the Lord. When I was growing up in the East End of London, nearly everyone in our area supported a football team called West Ham United. Every week, those fans would rally together and sing the club anthem, a song called 'you'll never walk alone'. Ironically for me, this was the ultimate revelation of the anointing.

I found that the greatest benefit of the anointing is to have God's presence walk with me all the time. The song that was our club anthem has become my daily song, I sing it to the beautiful Spirit who walks with me every day of my life. Jesus said the father never leaves him because he always does the things that please him (John 8:29). Wouldn't it be great for that to be our confession today? Wouldn't it be great that we should know of a surety that our Father walks with us perpetually? This may seem arrogant, but I believe that every believer should be able to make that claim, because of the mystery of the blood of Jesus Christ, which by the way, is the title of my next book by God's grace.

I would like to leave you with a poem, given to me by the Lord himself, whist on a ministry trip to Canada a few years ago. It really sums up the power of the anointing on my life, and hope it will inspire you to walk in the miracle which was the mystery of Christ, now revealed to you and I.

I pray that this will be a blessing to you. Enjoy

To the beautiful Spirit who walks with me

Who allows me to know, things that I cannot see

Who watches my slumber and wakes me in time

Who guides me to safely, each time after time

Who watches my habits, with warnings so clear

Who heightens my senses, when danger is near

Who is never too busy, to give me some time

And who always reminds me, that blessings are mine

Who gives me assurance, of heavenly peace

Whose love and attention, is never to cease

Who chooses my colours and sizes and style

Who sends me to work or relax for a while

Who handles relations, with steady true hands

Who when all are distant, the nearer he stands

Who never accuses. Who died for my sin

Who attentively listens to what I'm thinking

Who when I am praying, directs what to speak

Who fills me with power, each time I am weak

Who gently assures me, that I am his Son

Who firmly announces, the battle is Won

Who speaks in a language, unfruitful to me

Who lifts up a standard, to barricade Sea

Who quickens my thinking and makes things so clear

Who makes education much simpler to bear

Who brings my attention, to detail of life

Who keeps me from anger, from panic and strife

Who's always providing, some way or some how

Who gave me the words that you're reading right now

Who walks with me daily, I said at the start

Who is it? It's Jesus, the Christ in my Heart

Amen

Firstly I would like to give thanks to God for making me the man I am today. I also wish to say a huge thank you to:

Seva Jackman (My wife), our daughters Janah and Penny, Clive, Miles, Bailey and Hanson Hughes Graham, Bernice Wallace, Imogene Smith (Sis), Maria (Mum) and Percy Griffith, House of Victory Wellingborough. Pastor Benny and Sandy Thomas, Bishop Al Baxter, (Thanks for the mentorship) Bishop Junior and Pastor Lorraine Buchanan, (My confidant) Bishop John Francis, (Thanks for the word) Pastor Andrew Adeleke, Pastor Rick Johnston, (Thanks for my wife) Howard and Lesley Conder, (My TV pastors) Gordon and Lorna Pettie, Tim Vince, John Campbell (My revelation TV Bible study partners) Deborah Sweetin, (Prophetess) Pastor Richard Odoch, (Thanks for the anointing!) Pastor David Opakwrot, Aunt Esther and Brother Steed, (My early guides) Manna, Simone Stewart and the Stewart family, Karri Gerrard, Hector Cormack, Mark Powell, Tony Rich (Now dearly departed), Steve Carmichael (my Christ influence), Steve Voss, Eric and Deborah Skeete, (my friends) Bishop Carlton and Pastor Janet Morgan, Rick and Liz Osbourne, (Bible Study Buddies) Jocelyn Williams (eyes), The Bernard family, Sandra, Robert and the Wilsons, (HOV Comrades) Bishop Paul Archer, Bishop Dr Joe Ibojie, (Dream Doctor) Pastor Ionie Shas, (Pillar) Pastor Jennifer Clarke Singh, Ivyn Francis, Pastor Errol Henry, Pastor Tony Hill,

Camille and Billy Joe Cummings, (True Worshipper) My brothers Franklyn and Graceston Jackman, All of the family in Barbados, Whitfield and Shirley Jackman, Lee and Joe Grant, Pastor Ian McCormack, Pastor Philip Noel (My encourager), Pastor Hugh Osgood, Terry Quinn, The Chandlers, Sharon Palmer, Roger Samuels, Charles and Abigail Tamakloe.

I love you all with all my heart...

And for the dynamic influence of anointed preachers in the Body today, including Charles Capps, Creflo Dollar, Kenneth E. Hagin (late) Kenneth Copeland, John Bevere, Benny Thomas, Joseph Prince and Dr Leroy Thompson Snr.

I kept these with me for many years as I studied the anointing). This is exactly as I had them stapled to the back of my Bible.

Acts	10:38	God anointed Jesus
		God the anointer
Luke	4:18	After the baptism
		Jesus the anointed
Isaiah	61:1	The spirit of the lord
		Is the anointing
1 John	4:2	Spirit of antichrist
Luke	4:34	Come to destroy us?
		You have authority
Mark	5:7	I adjure you by God
		Demons are illegal
Matthew	17:5	Hear ye him
		God sent his word
2 Cor	5:18	The reconciliation
		We heard the word
2 Cor	1:21	God has anointed us
		God the anointer
1 John	2:27	The anointing received
		We are anointed

John	1:11	As many as received him
		We are his sons too
John	15:7	The word abides in you
		The word lives in you
1 Sam	10:6	Anointing changes you
		Word changes you
Psalm	89:20	Effects of
		Anointing establishes you
Psalm	92:10	Eyes and ears
		The word empowers you
Eph	1:3	All spiritual blessings are in the anointing
Gal	3:27	Abraham's seed
		We are heirs of God
Acts	8:5	Phillip preached Christ in Samaria
Acts	9:20	Paul preached Christ
Acts	10:37	Peter preached Christ
		Italian Cornelius
Mark	2:2	Jesus preached the word signs followed
Mark	16:20	Disciples preached God confirmed it

2 Tim	4:2	Preach the word by Paul's command
Acts	10:44	The holy ghost fell on all who heard
Heb	4:2	The word mixed belief or faith
1 Peter	1:23	Perfect birth The word is perfect
Prov	4:22	Health to our flesh Word dominates
John	6:63	My words are Spirit and life words
Gen	9:4	Life in the blood
Luke	1:38	Be it unto me said Mary
Luke	2:40	The child grew in spirit
John	1:3	Born of the spirit Spirit & life in blood
1 John	5:6	Water-blood - spirit Flesh-word - spirit

All Scriptures are quoted in NKJV: "Scripture taken from the New King James Version®. Copyright ©1982 by Thomas Nelson, Inc. Used by permission."

Authors note: We have chosen not to capitalise 'satan' or 'lucifer' within this publication, this is not a grammatical error.

About the Author

Hugh Alexander Jackman and his wife Seva are the Senior Pastors of House of Victory in Wellingborough, Northamptonshire.

His personal ministry was inspired by several Word of Faith and Prophetic Ministries. His calling has been summed up by Author and Spiritual Father Benny Thomas as being a Minister of the Prophetic Word of Faith.

Early in his ministry, God propelled him into International Television, where he aided in the birth and development of three Christian TV stations including Revelation TV, where he received some notoriety.

More recently, God has begun to use him significantly in the area of both teaching and preaching his anointed Word with signs and wonders following. As he lays his hands and declares the Prophetic Word of Faith, God is bringing healing and deliverance to many.

Other materials by this author are available at:

www.houseofvictory.org.uk

UK: 01933 426354

International: +44 1933 426354

www.ingramcontent.com/pod-product-compliance
Lightning Source LLC
LaVergne TN
LVHW041540070426
835507LV00011B/841